HIGH SCHOOL SURVIVAL

**BY CURRENT HIGH SCHOOL STUDENTS
ACROSS THE COUNTRY
EDITED BY GREG GOTTESMAN, DANIEL BAER & FRIENDS**

Macmillan General Reference

A Pearson Education Macmillan Company
1633 Broadway
New York, NY 10019-6785

Macmillan Publishing books may be purchased for business or sales promotional use. For information, please write: Special Markets Department, Macmillan Publishing USA, 1633 Broadway, New York, NY 10019.

An Arco Book

ARCO and colophon is a registered trademark of Macmillan USA

MACMILLAN and colophon is a registered trademark of Macmillan USA

Manufactured in the United States of America

10 9 8 7 6 5 4 3 2 1

Library of Congress Number: 99-63230

ISBN: 0-02863250-8

To Alita Kiaer and Ruth Newman, the two best high school teachers I ever had. GG

For Joan, Steve, and Artis, three people who are not family but who acted as such when we needed them. DBB

Table of Contents

Acknowledgements

This book was written entirely by *current* high school students, and all the anecdotes are from *current* high school students. This is their book. Daniel Baer and I had the privilege of editing (as little as possible) their sometimes funny, sometimes corny, always down-to-earth and insightful work. The contributing student-authors (and the chapter(s) each one worked on) include: Christine Annenberg (Chapter 10, "Computers and the Internet"), Merritt Baer (Chapter 5, "Homework: A Necessary Evil"; and Chapter 22, "Dealing with Parents"), Peter Baer (Chapter 16, "Dating in High School"), Lauren Baum (Chapter 11, "Athletics"), Marc Bridge (Chapter 21, "Time Management"), Nathan Burstein (Chapter 9, "Choosing Classes"), Leah Carnick (Chapter 2, "The First Day"), Mike Carnick (Chapter 2, "The First Day"), Annie Chu (Chapter 23, "Nutrition: Eating Right and Living Right in High School"), Stephanie Curry (Chapter 1, "Letting Go of Middle School"), Jennifer Deryuen (Chapter 12, "Extracurriculars: A Salvation from the Grind"), Miriam D'Jaen (Chapter 6, "Essay Writing: Dirty Work, but We All Have to Do It"), Meredith Hagashi (Chapter 14, "Community Service"), Mike Hazel (Chapter 24, "Preparing for Standardized Tests"), Shannon Hopkins (Chapter 18, "Alcohol and Drugs"), P.J. Hoyt (Chapter 3, "New Classes"), Julie Mallory (Chapter 7, "Tests: A Nightmare, True or False?"), Susan Rindlaub (Chapter 15, "Friends"), Casey Rose (Chapter 17, "Prom, Homecoming, and Other Dances"), Sara Shulman (Chapter 8, "Teachers: Friends or Foes?"), Kate Sommers-Dawes (Chapter 20, "Fashion and Shopping"), Orlando Tirado (Chapter 13, "Working in School"), Jason Uhrmacher (Chapter 25, "College Application Process"), Ajay Vashee (Chapter 4, "New Expectations: Getting Accustomed to High School Life), and Mike Wahl (Chapter 19, "Cars").

We also need to thank the many current high school students across the country who contributed personal stories to individual chapters to make this book more accessible and more real. You are the heart and soul of the following pages.

The one high school student who deserves special mention is Merritt Baer. Merritt, who is finishing up her freshman year at Heritage High School in Colorado, wrote two chapters, edited all 25 chapters, and played a key administrative role during the process. If you hear a tiny voice as you read through the various chapters, it is probably Merritt's.

We also want to single out for thanks Kerin Lubetich of Mercer Island High School in Washington for her humorous and witty cartoons. Kerin worked without complaint under a tight deadline. You can see the great results.

The one teacher most responsible for this book is Jan Sayers, an English teacher from Mercer Island High School. Jan rounded up her most gifted students and put them to work on this project. Her influence is all over the writing in this book. Jan takes dedication to her students to new heights each year—we need more teachers like Jan.

Daniel Baer, the better half of this team of editors, worked tirelessly to make sure that this book was something special and different. Dan, I think we did it.

Our editors at ARCO also deserve special mention for their incredible contribution to this book. Editing high school student writing is not easy, especially if you are trying hard to keep the flavor of the student writing intact. Stephanie Hammett, managing editor; Don Essig, acquisitions editor; and Karen Reinisch, director of publishing, have worked hard on the editing side and have been very patient with us throughout the process. We have enjoyed working with such a great team. Linda Bernbach, a former editor at ARCO, was the first to agree to publish this book, and we thank her for her enthusiasm and great work.

Finally, I want to thank my family, especially my mother and grandmother, who were so pivotal in the first book of this series, *College Survival*. My best friend and wife, Shannon, is the person most responsible for the energy behind this book. We came up with the idea of high school students writing to other high school students as we walked through Harvard Yard together on a frosty winter day several years ago. We met Dan there, too, to combine forces. It's not the greatest idea ever conjured up in Harvard Yard, but hopefully it's a pretty good one. . . .

Greg Gottesman

Few books are created by one person alone, but this project has been a group effort from the start. The many high school students from around the country who helped put the material together deserve not only my thanks, but also my congratulations on a job well done.

It has not been easy to juggle this project along with ever copious amounts of schoolwork, and it would not be an overstatement to say that I owe my sanity to my roommates David and Conan. Of course, they do much more than provide sanity; they are also my family, my home away from home, and I thank them for being that.

I want to thank Ken and Nancy Atkinson for their love and guidance through the years. They are *good* people, in the fullest sense of the word, and I appreciate their efforts to make me so, too. Thanks to my teachers and friends at HHS, and now at Harvard. Special thanks to my mentors: Abby Rezneck, Victoria Cain, Zac Eller, Trafford Welden, and Anthony Appiah.

And, of course, my greatest debt now and always shall be to my family. Mom and Dad have been my anchor in spite of the storms that they themselves have weathered over the past few years. My brother, Peter, is the object of my most sincere admiration—our relationship is the source of many lessons for me. My sister, Merritt, humbles me with her intellect, humors me with her wit, and enriches me with her commitment to good. She worked tirelessly on this project, and, as usual, did so without complaint. As for little Lyle, though you are still too young to read this, when you can you will know that it is the joy that you have brought to all of us that has been the greatest gift of our lives.

Daniel Baer

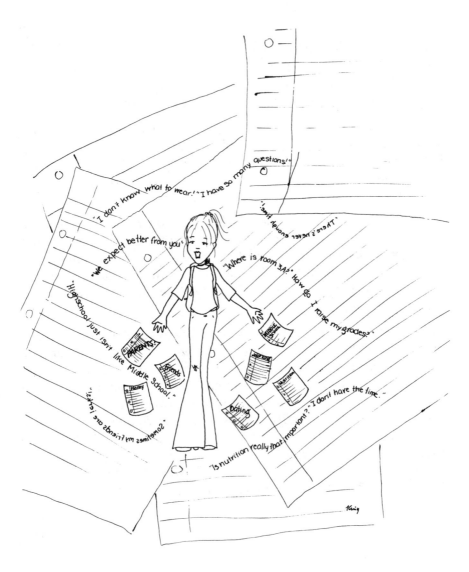

Preface

"All our dreams come true—if we have the courage to pursue them."

—WALT DISNEY

Have you ever heard a friend say something like, "I wish I was back in the first grade—life was so much easier then"? Have you ever thought it yourself? Ah, to revisit the times when math class consisted of playing with multishaped, multicolored building blocks, and when English meant using crayons to color in the pictures that matched the words.

But, all sentimental reflections aside, those days are over. Presumably, you're reading this book because you're in high school now, or at least on your way in the near future. High schools don't have multicolored blocks, and unless you have that senile American history teacher who makes you color maps, you almost never get to use crayons. It's a whole new ball game: The classes are tougher, the teachers no longer act like they are also your mother, and life in general gets a whole lot busier.

This book, written by high school kids from all around the country, will not give you all the answers to the various challenges of high school life. What it will give you are facts, accurate information, and alternatives. The following chapters are filled with the tricks of the trade that our authors learned the hard way—so that you don't have to. This book will teach you how to cajole your English teacher into granting you an extension, and it will help you plan for your first prom. It will give you tips on keeping up with fashion without a big budget and will offer strategies for keeping up with homework when you don't have a lot of time. *Please do not read every page.* Skip around to the chapters and sections that interest you most. Read the stories. Save some chapters for later.

The students who have written the chapters of this book have compiled the best advice available to help you get the most out of your high school experience. High school comes with a host of new responsibilities, but brings you even more great opportunities. Fasten your seatbelt, because it's bound to be a wild ride. Hopefully, this book will help you through the ups and downs along the way.

Remember what Abraham Lincoln said, "The best thing about the future is that it comes only one day at a time." Take high school one day at a time. Don't forget that success in high school depends on one thing more than anything else: attitude. High school is not easy, but it is not rocket science either. Look at all the people you know who have graduated. You will get there. Have fun, and take some time to smell the roses along the way.

CHAPTER 1

Letting Go of Middle School

> *Just when I was starting to get used to middle school, I was off to high school. My mom drove my older brother and me the first day and dropped us off in front of school. All the kids at high school looked bigger than I was. The building was big and the hallways were long. I remember getting to school early and seeing my friend in the cafeteria. We bought some donuts and chomped them down—we were both nervous. Looking back now, I can't believe we were so scared. After the first few weeks, the high school didn't seem so big anymore. I settled in and forgot about why I was so nervous. Everyone settles in eventually. You will, too.*
>
> —JASON, MERCER ISLAND HIGH SCHOOL,
> MERCER ISLAND, WASHINGTON

The days of the milk-money bullies are finally over. Instead, you find yourself facing the next era of your life: high school. Some people have been waiting for this moment ever since they started seventh grade. Others are not yet ready to leave the familiarity of middle school behind. While there is no right or wrong attitude, you do have the power to make this transition as easy or as hard as you like.

Whether you look at the next four years with excitement or dread, the first few days of high school are scary for everyone. Facing the unknown isn't easy. Some anxieties—such as wondering whether you will be able to find your classes and being afraid of whether older students will pick on you—are common. Keep in mind, however, that they are only *temporary*. By enduring those first few days, you will have conquered one of your biggest obstacles: fear. And you know what? Everybody makes it through those first days.

Some challenges of high school are longer lasting. Worries such as complex social problems and academic strain are a recurring part of the experience. While you may never escape these problems, you can learn how to live with them. Being able to handle these obstacles is the real trick to surviving high school—and that's the reason this book was written. Some of the things mentioned in this chapter—homework, classes, teachers, activities, and so on—will have entire chapters devoted to them later in the book. This chapter is a general overview, just to get you thinking.

THE DIFFERENCES BETWEEN MIDDLE SCHOOL AND HIGH SCHOOL

> *In high school, you are exposed to a lot of new issues such as drugs, alcohol, and sex that were never problems in middle school.*
>
> —Lydia, Theodore Roosevelt High School, Des Moines, Iowa
>
> *You have a lot more freedom and fewer restrictions, but you also have more responsibility. There are also more opportunities to explore your interests.*
>
> —Matt, University School of Jackson, Jackson, Tennessee

> *In middle school, the littlest things were a big deal. In high school, the petty things don't matter as much anymore.*
>
> —COURTNEY, ROOSEVELT HIGH SCHOOL, SEATTLE, WASHINGTON
>
> *You get to meet different kinds of people and people who are in different grades.*
>
> —KARA, MERCER ISLAND HIGH SCHOOL, MERCER ISLAND, WASHINGTON

ACADEMIC DIFFERENCES

Grades Matter Now

When you got your report card in middle school, you either hid it from your parents or you tacked it up on the refrigerator. After a few months, it probably got thrown into a junk pile, from which it soon disappeared forever. In high school, however, this is not the case. From now on, the grades that you receive are permanently recorded on your transcript. Future employers or colleges look at this transcript, so unlike in middle school, you have to live with the consequences of slacking off. Make time for homework and studying. No, it is not fun, but it is probably beneficial to your future.

Note to the overachievers: While it is important to make time for schoolwork, you should not devote your life to getting a 4.0. You will face pressure to do well, but don't blow it out of proportion. Fight the urge to be overly dramatic: One "C" grade on a test does not mean that you will end up flipping burgers for the rest of your life. Do the best that you can, and make time for the things that are most important to you, such as friends, family, and after-school activities.

You Can Pick Many of Your Courses

As in middle school, you still have to sit through that boring math class. However, you now have more opportunities to spice up your schedule with electives. If you are interested in debate as opposed to ceramics, you will likely now have the ability to follow that path. You may still have requirements to fulfill, but you at least have more choice in how and when you get it all done.

Another aspect of this involves picking the level of courses you take. Intrigued by taking all honors classes? You now have that option. If, however, you hate science and want very little to do with it in your future career, then you don't have to take the most challenging science course available. Keep in mind, however, that even though you might think you have a career path chosen, you could always change your mind—don't limit yourself. Take the opportunity to try out for a play, take a Shakespeare class, learn about painting, or even learn how to cook. You never know what you'll end up liking or what skills you might use in your future career.

High School Means More Homework

Regardless of the level of difficulty of your classes, you will notice a change in workload. The work you receive may increase in amount and difficulty, but it is not impossible to get decent grades. Yes, you will be challenged, but teachers do not set you up to fail.

Plan on spending more time on homework in high school than you did in middle school. This means that managing your time is more crucial in high school. If you are trying to juggle a job, cross-country meets, and band practice, then you need to plan time for homework. If you are constantly overwhelmed with demands from both school and outside obligations, you may have to consider dropping an activity.

SOCIAL DIFFERENCES

Welcome to the Bottom of the Totem Pole

When you left middle school, you were the oldest. People respected and feared you. If you wanted to sit at *that* lunch table, then the sixth- or seventh-graders moved to accommodate you. Not so in high school. You are now at the bottom of the ladder, referred to by the upperclassmen as "little freshmen." This title includes making an occasional fool of yourself for the sake of a senior, otherwise known as *hazing*. Hazing is more of a right of initiation than torture, but sometimes a senior may go too far. Know your limit, and know when someone is overstepping his or her bounds. Putting someone in a garbage can is bad enough; putting the lid on the can is going way too far. While you may not feel comfortable tattling to a teacher or an administrator, you can at least ask for advice on how you can handle the situation.

Serious hazing problems do happen, but they are very rare. About 99 percent of the time, seniors are great to have as older mentors. It is comforting (and also fun) to have someone to look up to and some-one who will look out for you. Try to make friends with some upperclassmen.

You Will Meet Lots of New People

The best part about your high school years will be the people who fill them. While there is that chance that you will remain best friends with your kindergarten buddy, your circle of friends will most likely change and expand. Your closest friends throughout high school will probably be people that you didn't know before you got to high school. Introduce yourself to new faces, and don't blow off opportunities to meet new people. You may also find that because your classes now include people from different grades, you have the chance to get to know upperclassmen. Your junior lab partner could very well turn out to be one of your closest friends.

Enjoy Your New Freedom

Finally! Your parents have given you a later curfew, and you have friends who can drive. High school is what you have been waiting for! More freedom, more fun, right? Right! The next four years can be some of the greatest of your life, so make them the best that you can.

However, there is a tricky side to this. Your parents, who are giving you more freedom, are also displaying more trust in you. Violating this trust by doing something stupid (or illegal) can have very messy consequences. That late curfew may be drastically cut short, and you may find yourself unable to enjoy other privileges. All of a sudden, high school's potential for unlimited fun is suddenly . . . well, limited. But the hardest thing about it will be rebuilding the trust between you and your parents. So before you decide to do something that may violate that trust, remember the value of your newly acquired freedom.

What About Drugs, Alcohol, and Sex?

You may have had contact with some issues such as drugs, alcohol, and sex in middle school, but it was most likely the tip of the iceberg. In high school, you will find that these issues are much more pronounced. They affect everyone, either directly or indirectly. Perhaps you are the one experimenting with alcohol or drugs, or maybe you are surrounded by friends who are. Whatever decisions you make regarding these issues, you have to live with yourself the next morning—and for the rest of your life. Don't get so caught up with needing to belong that you wind up doing something that makes you feel uncomfortable. You may be surprised to discover that people respect you even more for saying no to some things rather than always following the crowd.

You Have a Clean Slate!

One of the greatest things about going to a new school is that no one knows about the time you were caught picking your nose in class, or the time in fifth grade when your teacher was your best and only friend.

> *I was so glad when I got to high school. I had been at the same school for nine years, and I never stopped hearing about the time in second grade when I chased all the guys around, yelling and trying to kiss them. I was so sick of everybody knowing every story, and I just really wanted to start over and make my own memories, to get a new reputation other than being boy-crazy.*
>
> —ALISON, EAST HIGH SCHOOL, DENVER, COLORADO

High school is your opportunity to change your reputation, to get a new image, to have a fresh start. If you are tired of being thought of as a ditz by former teachers, now is your chance to start a new reputation for yourself in a place where the staff doesn't know your previous record.

Social reputations can be tricky to change, however. It's easy to get a bad reputation fast—and it's hard to salvage a good reputation afterward. Don't blow it when people are just getting to know you. First impressions are very important, and you'll be making a lot of them right away. Just remember to be yourself, and try not to get weirded-out so that you act completely different to seem cool. Everyone gets sick of people like that.

Cliques Are Part of High School

To some extent, every high school must deal with cliques. You'll find the athletes, the science-nerds, the fringe-people, and so on. It's nice to belong to a certain group, but cliques can be extremely exclusive and hurtful. Don't be afraid to go outside your circle of friends and socialize with different kinds of people. Other people will admire you for being inclusive. Also don't feel that you have to belong to one clique: If you can make lots of different friends, you will always have someone to turn to when you're mad at or hurt by a friend or two.

MAKING THE TRANSITION

> *In my freshman year of high school, I was involved in band. We began practicing a month before school started, so I had a great chance to meet new people. By the time the first day of school started, I found myself saying "hi" to all the people I met through band that summer. Getting involved in my school really helped me to make the transition.*
>
> —JILLIAN VINEY, MORTON HIGH SCHOOL, MORTON, ILLINOIS

GET INVOLVED

High school has something for everyone, regardless of their interests: sports, music, art, or after-school clubs. By getting involved in an activity of some kind, you interact with people who share the same interests as you. The bonds you form with people as a team are unlike those of other friendships. You share the same experiences and triumphs (such as, "we kicked that team's butt"). One of the best things about high school is that it is probably bigger and more diverse than your middle school. You will have more opportunities, so take advantage of them! Get involved in sports or student council and find people who share similar interests with you; there are bound to be kindred spirits out there, so take the initiative and get involved. You'll thank yourself later.

KEEP AN OPEN MIND

As much as you may have heard from older siblings and friends, you really don't know what high school will be like for you. Keep an open mind as to what you expect: It's very easy to be misled and become disappointed.

The hardest part about having an open mind is keeping it positive. How you see high school determines the kinds of experiences you have in it. Of course, the fact that you are reading this book implies that you want to do well and that you want to get through high school without having regrets.

DON'T JUDGE PEOPLE

When you walk into your first period class and the guy who sits in front of you is mostly tattoos and has a red mohawk, you are probably going to develop some initial judgments. You will also make judgments about the girl with Abercrombie™ price tags sticking out all over the place, and the girl who makes Victoria's Secret™ models look conservative. Trust me, everyone does this, but try to refrain from making harsh judgments, as this will limit your list of potential friends. Respect and tolerance are essential; stay away from judgments based on race, religion, clothes, or pretty much anything else. Many people use high school as an opportunity to find their style, and physical appearance is a creative outlet. You may want to do this also, so keep in mind that if you pierced every facial feature, people will make ignorant judgments about you, too. Try to accept people as they are: Although it might sound cliché, it really is what's on the inside that counts.

MAKE TIME FOR YOURSELF

With all the new academic requirements and social opportunities, you can easily become overwhelmed. Your attitude of "high school is awesome" may change to "high school is hell" in a hurry. If you want to survive the four years of high school with your sanity intact, however, make some time for yourself. Whether you mindlessly take the dog for a walk or sleep all day, plan downtime when you don't have to think about anything related to school.

No matter how independent you are, the transition to high school is a lot harder to make on your own. During some of the first days of school, you will feel insecure or lost in the shuffle. This is when you need your friends to keep you going. Remember to shoot hoops with a pal or gossip over the phone, and don't feel guilty about indulging yourself when you really need it. Sure, you're saving up for a car, but it's okay to buy that awesome new CD. The key is balance so that you don't feel neglected but that you also aren't dropping everything so that you can do whatever you want to do.

If You Just Can't Let Go of Middle School . . .

> *When I left middle school, I did not want to go to high school. I didn't make the transition to high school because I didn't want to. As a result of my bad attitude, I wasted the first few months of my freshman year. Then I realized that I wasn't going back, and I had to make the best of what I had. I still haven't made the full transition, but day by day it is getting better. While I still miss the familiarity of middle school, I am finally seeing the positive side of high school.*
>
> —Christie, Desert Mountain High School, Scottsdale, Arizona

Perhaps you've moved to a new city, or you simply wish for the good old days of middle school to return. Either way, you are probably missing the familiarity of your old school. It's okay to miss old friends and traditions, but living in the past won't get you anywhere in the present. Try to make your high school familiar in its own way so that you can eventually feel that you belong to your new school. Hopefully you'll totally fit in and you'll have a blast, but just in case you're experiencing a case of middle school sickness, bear these two helpful hints in mind.

GO BACK TO VISIT IF YOU WANT

> *I was really excited to leave middle school because of all the usual shallow reasons; I thought that high school would be so awesome with more friends, more guys, more fun. High school has been fun, but I also find myself actually missing middle school. Going back to visit has helped a lot because I can see my teachers and just feel comfortable again in a familiar setting.*
>
> —Holly, East High School, Denver, Colorado

You never thought that you would miss that old cafeteria smell, but lately you have been homesick for anything that represents middle school. Perhaps all you need is a final opportunity to say another good-bye. Drop in to visit old teachers, or walk down those musty hallways. Keep in mind that you may be remembering middle school for something it isn't. Those good old days are never as great as you remember them to be.

FOCUS ON THE POSITIVE

Make a list of the positive aspects of high school. "Well, what if I can't think of any?" Force yourself. Ask other friends what they like best about high school. Maybe they are seeing something you're not. By focusing on the positive, you are less likely to dwell on the negative. You can even try taping your list to the bathroom mirror or someplace else where it can be a constant reminder.

Transitions Aren't Easy . . .

High school is a balance between school and social activities, sanity and stress, laughter and tears. Whether or not these are the best years of your life is up to you. So have fun, learn a lot, and carpe diem! (For those of you who haven't seen the movie *Dead Poets Society,* carpe diem means "seize the day.") So it's a little cheesy, but rent the movie and you'll see what we mean. Seize the day.

CHAPTER 2

The First Day

It was my first day of really being a high-schooler! I was psyched! This is when the fun begins, when you forget about the immature guys you've been in classes with since fourth grade and about the time you were caught picking your nose in class. Goodbye, middle school! I was ready, I was feeling fine. I had gotten the perfect ensemble to wear that first crucial day. This was the day, right? Umm, well kinda. I strutted up the steps, Little Miss Confident. And then, as I watched all these kids around me slapping each other on the back and talking and laughing, it hit me: I am a freshman. And maybe the guys here are going to be some of the same ones I grew up with. And maybe math here isn't going to be all-dependent on late-night study sessions with cute seniors. This is just school.

Of course, after this realization, I did go on to have an awesome ninth-grade year, but it was hard at first to deal with going from a Big Dude On Campus as an eighth-grader to lowly freshman status. Still, I know that next year I'll walk in to the first day with all my friends, just the way last year's sophomores did.

—Jenni, Heritage High School, Littleton, Colorado

In the words of a great musical artist, "You all ready for this?" It's not "the end of the world as we know it," but for many, the first day of high

school is the day when you officially become a teen, a rite of passage that bridges the gap between childhood and adulthood. The first day can be very intimidating, but not to worry—it gets easier with time, trust us. All those unknown faces in the hallway eventually will turn into acquaintances, so just get over those initial blues and think, "I will survive!"

The following 15 tips will ease the process of entering into some of the most important years in your school career. Read on, and don't be afraid! Everyone goes through the initial anxiety, but it's not as bad as you think.

The first day of high school, I came in thinking that this year would be the beginning of the rest of my life. Here was where it gets good, I thought. As if just belonging in high school halls could change everything. But actually, I found that high school isn't much different from any transition, and it definitely wasn't worth all the hype. I mean, yeah, it was cool that there was a club for everything you ever dreamed of, but my friends were the same kind of people and my classes were basically the same. It was not that big of a deal, and it wasn't worth the time I spent thinking about how totally different it would be.

—MERRITT, HERITAGE HIGH SCHOOL, LITTLETON, COLORADO

1. GET A GOOD NIGHT'S SLEEP.

Although it's hard to sleep, it is important that you are adequately rested for the long day ahead of you. It's natural to feel excited and anxious, and you may have to force yourself to close your eyes. If you absolutely cannot sleep, lie down and read a book or watch some TV until you feel drowsy enough to sleep. Don't drink caffeine before you go to bed: When you're coming from a summer vacation of staying up late and sleeping in, it will be hard to go to bed early, but it is vital that you discipline yourself to try to get at least eight hours of sleep. Going to high school tired can be a hellish experience.

2. BRING A LUNCH THE FIRST DAY.

Some cafeteria food is supposedly quite tasty, but we haven't found it yet. Many school cafeterias specialize in meals that are barely edible—don't chance it on the first day. The best thing to do is to brown-bag it for the first week, until you know when and what the cafeteria offers and what looks decent—and not so decent.

3. PLAN TO MEET SOME FRIENDS AT LUNCH.

If you have some friends who you know will be at school, plan to meet them at lunch. It can be very comforting to see some familiar faces among a sea of strangers, and you will be surprised at how much a brief meeting of the minds can help make the first day seem funnier and less anxiety-filled. Talking and laughing about your new teachers, classes, and classmates is a great way to spend your first lunch.

4. BE PREPARED.

Usually, high school teachers do not send home a supply list. On the first day of school each teacher likely will tell you what he or she would like you to have for that specific class. Do not come to school empty-handed, however. Bring a notebook, perhaps a folder, and a pen and pencil, and you should have all that you need until your teachers tell you otherwise. You might also want to bring a calendar or notebook to write down homework assignments, although your workload will probably be pretty light for the first week.

5. MEMORIZE YOUR BUS NUMBER AND SCHEDULE.

If you are riding the big yellow bus, find out which one you ride, where it picks you up, and where it drops you off. Remember, too, that you might have a different bus in the afternoon than in the morning. And make sure you are on time: Nine times out of ten, the bus driver will not wait for you.

I normally did not ride the bus, but one particular afternoon I needed to. I did not know my bus number, though, and ended up missing it. Fortunately, there was another bus that passed my neighborhood, so I took that one, but it dropped me off a mile and a half away from my house. On a hot afternoon in boots, with my extremely heavy backpack on my shoulders and after being at school all day, that was not when I would have liked to get my exercise. But, now I know my bus schedule, just in case I have to ride it again.

—LEAH, CHAPEL HILL HIGH SCHOOL, CHAPEL HILL, NORTH CAROLINA

6. KNOW YOUR SURROUNDINGS.

Your high school campus may seem like a monolithic catacomb of twisting halls, with classroom numbers reaching up into the triple digits. Don't worry—it is completely natural to feel lost the first few days. Even though it might be hard to fathom, you will eventually get used to the layout and it will become like your second home. Make sure you pick up a map, if your school offers one, and if you get lost, don't be ashamed to ask for directions (believe us, everyone has experienced getting lost the first day). If your school offers an orientation, by all means make sure to attend it before school starts; this will greatly aid you when you're trying to find your classrooms. Keep a lookout for where the library, cafeteria, and other important locations are as you walk around school.

7. FIND OUT WHERE YOUR CLASSES ARE AND WHO YOUR TEACHERS ARE BEFORE SCHOOL.

You should be familiar with where your classes are and who your teachers are before the first day of school. You don't want to walk in late the first day of class, if you can help it.

The one impression I remember having of my high school during my first day was that it was huge. I guess I've finally grown into it after four years, but doing so wasn't easy. During my first day there, I got lost more times than I can remember. We had a freshman orientation where students led us around the school, but none of it had really sunk in. I think it's important to pay attention to whatever kind of orientation you get at your school (most, if not all, have them) because once they let you loose that first day, you're on your own. It's not like no one will help you or give you directions, but it's your responsibility to ask—and that took me a while to get used to. This was a big change for me because in middle school I was used to having at least one friend with whom I had most of my classes, and we'd walk to them together. In high school, you'll rarely have two classes in a row with the same person, so you have to get used to walking around by yourself. What I'm trying to get across is that it's good to know where your classes are before you throw yourself in with the crowds—once you're there, it's sometimes too intimidating to ask strangers how to get where you need to go.

—KARI, CHAPEL HILL HIGH SCHOOL, CHAPEL HILL,
NORTH CAROLINA

8. CHECK YOUR CLASS SCHEDULE.

The school system isn't perfect, and there is a small chance that your class schedule will be incorrectly issued. One of your teachers might be wrong, or you may have duplicate or missing class periods. You'll probably end up hearing about someone who had three PE classes on her schedule, or some students who were even missing a couple class periods. If you see such an error, inform your counselor as soon as possible. Don't feel bad if you see an error; it happens to a lot of people and is easily corrected. Don't wait because you think you won't get caught with three missing class periods or multiple PE classes: You *will* get caught eventually and probably will end up having to make up any homework you missed.

9. KNOW WHERE YOUR LOCKER IS AND HOW TO GET TO IT.

Some schools assign you a locker before school starts, and others issue assignments the first week of school. Find out how your school works and whether your school provides a lock. If it doesn't, find out if the school cares which kind of lock—combination or key lock—you get. Your locker will be your home away from home, and you'll want to protect it.

10. BE FAMILIAR WITH ANY DRESS CODES AND OTHER GENERAL RULES.

Understanding all the rules is to your advantage. That way, you will not unknowingly break them—or, if you do break the rules, you will at least know about it. If you come to school wearing something that does not fall within the dress code, the faculty will probably send you home or make you wear either your gym clothes or clothes from the lost-and-found—neither is probably part of that special look you were going for on the first day!

> *With a month of high school under my belt, I set out to struggle free from the suffocating social structure of my school, proudly marching down the hallway in beer-advertising, bra-strap-showing outfits. I was soon stopped by an assistant principal in the middle of my parade to fourth period. Brought into his harshly lit cubicle, I sweated out the worst of his lecture about how the dress code can bring a sense of dignity and how I should be more willing to obey his demands. Although I was civil to the man, I went away from his Glade-scented prison unchanged.*
>
> *For awhile after this incident with the school administrator, I wore the same shredded jeans and revealing tops as before, happy to have my personal*

> *style still intact. It wasn't until I was almost sent home for a particularly tight outfit that I realized that the assistant principal had meant business. Grudgingly donning a grimy, oversized man's shirt from the lost-and-found, I spent the rest of the day in misery, my idiosyncrasy having been stepped upon and shrouded under someone's forgotten rags.*
>
> —Betty, Chapel Hill High School, Chapel Hill, North Carolina

11. Get advice.

If you have any friends or older siblings that have gone through their first year of high school, consult them for advice about the coming year. Although some may delight in telling you horror stories of freshmen getting canned and teachers that give tests once a week, you will likely find some useful information on which teachers and classes are good and which are not so good. And maybe they'll clue you in on ways to avoid the potential pitfalls of the first day.

12. Learn about your teachers.

Each teacher will have a different perspective on what is most important in his or her class. Some might put the most stress on tests, while others may have a passion for note taking. In any case, it is very important that you find out what each teacher expects from you. On the first day, the teacher often will pass out a sheet of paper highlighting all the important rules and how much weight homework and tests will have on your grade. If you have any special needs, such as sitting close to the blackboard in order to see, you should clear this up with the teacher at the end of the class—he or she should be more than happy to accommodate you.

13. Check for extracurricular activities.

While you are braving the rapids of your first few days of high school, keep your eyes and ears out for any clubs and activities that you may be interested in joining. Listen closely to announcements and read school bulletins for times and schedules. Extracurricular activities can be a great way to meet new people. (Check out Chapter 12, "Extracurriculars: A Salvation from the Grind," later in the book.)

If you have a particular interest in a club or activity, consult your counselor, and he or she will provide you with the information you need. You should also look out for available tutoring that may take place after school; such help may be useful when report card time rolls around.

14. DON'T BE AFRAID TO ASK QUESTIONS.

Most teachers are teachers because they love to teach: They love to answer questions, so ask lots of them! Other kids probably have the same questions as you, so you are doing them a favor by asking. As another bonus, teachers usually know the school like the back of their hands, so if you do not know where your next class is, ask your teacher.

Also don't forget that older students were once where you are now. Many times they feel cool when you defer to their experience. So if you're lost, ask another student—you'll probably get a helpful answer and maybe a new friend.

15. TAKE SOME TIME TO SMELL THE ROSES.

The first week is a great time to meet new people and make new friends, but you don't have to feel obligated to know everyone or perform your best the first week. If you're the type that feels more comfortable becoming a fly on the wall and simply observing your new home, that's fine. The teachers will not assign heavy work the first few weeks, so don't worry about lots of homework right away. Get to know your teachers and the classes, and just concentrate on settling down in your new school.

ONE FINAL IMPORTANT TIP: DON'T BE INTIMIDATED!

Everyone is shy the first day of school. We convince ourselves that everyone else has more friends or is cooler than us, smarter than us, better looking, or more athletic. It's simply not true. Everyone is insecure that first day. Everyone is thinking similar insecure thoughts. High school is a time to make new friends and to experiment with new surroundings. Get out there and meet new people. Everyone will be anxious to make new friends, and they will appreciate your friendliness more than you know.

CHAPTER 3

New Classes

I couldn't wait to make the transition from middle school to high school—that meant more people, more dates, more opportunities; going to the Friday night football games; and being a part of the older crowd. I was looking forward to a lot of things with high school. The one thing that I didn't spend much time thinking about or preparing for was something I wish I would have: more classes, and much harder classes.

—PALMER, GRANGEVILLE HIGH SCHOOL, GRANGEVILLE, IDAHO

Gone are the days when you could happily twitter away the days in social studies as long as your sugar-cube pyramid fit well in your diorama. Alas, along with the exciting new life that awaits you in high school, you also get some real tough classes. Hopefully, the following tips will help you avoid some of the pitfalls of high school classes, a different animal than what you experienced in middle school or junior high.

1. CLASSES COUNT.

High school is very different—and pretty scary—because grades now count for both your grade point average and class rankings. Each and every high school class affects your GPA, and colleges care about your GPA. For most freshmen, there comes a sudden realization of, "You must be kidding me! I've got to work hard if I plan to go to college." But, hey, as long as you realize that these classes are important, then with the proper attitude you should have no problem succeeding.

Slacking off isn't as inconsequential as it was in middle school because now there are consequences for your actions—it's the real McCoy.

2. MAKE THE MOST OF YOUR CLASSES.

A definite change from middle school to high school is that you get to choose many of the classes you take. You will probably have two or three classes that you can't stand or that make you work so hard that by the end of the semester you're ready to blow a gasket. But the nice thing about high school is that if you play your cards right, you can create a varied schedule that's bearable—and even fun—if you choose classes that interest you.

You may have classes in high school that put you to sleep. For you, the sleepers will probably be classes in subject areas that don't interest you, such as math, or social studies, or perhaps art. Make the best of the situation—get some friends to sign up for the same period, and be enthusiastic. Who knows what hidden talents you have.

3. BRACE YOURSELF, BUT REMEMBER THAT EVERYONE'S IN THE SAME BOAT!

You will have to struggle through some of the core classes: algebra, chemistry, English literature—some of these classes are going to be really tough. While it's important to take these classes seriously and to be ready to devote more time and effort to each of them than you devoted to all your homework in middle school, remember that you're not fighting this battle alone. There will probably be at least 20 co-warriors in each of these battles. You'll make it through, and you may even learn a few things. Attitude is 90 percent of the battle, and you can choose to have a good attitude or a bad one. Above all, don't be scared of these classes; they are only as bad as you let them be.

4. DON'T BE COCKY.

> *As I look back now on entering high school, I was quite arrogant in classes. The best example is my biology class, where I felt I could debate my way out of anything. On tests, I would argue questions that really*

> *had no validity. I figured that if I put up a good fight and ranted and raved, I might get at least partial credit.*
>
> *What it really did was make the teacher mad because I thought I was smarter that he was, and I wasted class time (which isn't always a bad thing, but here it wasn't good). Since I argued every little thing, the teacher didn't exactly have a good opinion of me and, subsequently, didn't give me the benefit of the doubt in many instances.*
>
> —PALMER, GRANGEVILLE HIGH SCHOOL, GRANGEVILLE, IDAHO

High school can be a humbling or an ego-boosting experience. If you're leaning toward the "I'm all that and a bag of chips" attitude, just try to take it all in stride and not act too cocky; you still have a lot to learn, and no one—especially the teacher at the front of the room—likes arrogant know-it-alls. High school teachers want to help freshmen adjust to their new environment, and they can be really helpful if you let them. But if you come into the classroom with an ego the size of Texas, then a teacher is likely to think that the best thing he or she can do is to cut your ego down to size.

5. YOU NEVER GET A SECOND CHANCE TO MAKE A FIRST IMPRESSION.

Teachers probably won't have any idea who you are coming out of middle school. You will be one of many new freshman faces. It's a good idea to make yourself stand out a little to the teacher, in a good way. Usually, if you start out on the right foot, you'll be automatically considered "one of the good students"—and with any luck, you'll stay that way (and be able to get away with more later!).

Helpful Hints for Making a Positive Impression on Your New Teachers

(Also see Chapter 8, "Teachers: Friends or Foes?" for more tips.)

- Be friendly. There's a balance here: You want to be congenial, but not a kiss-up. Even if the class is really boring, if all your friends tell you it's a total nap class, and if the teacher is the Wicked Witch of the West, try to seem cordial. However, there's no need to get chummy and start walking your teacher's dog on Saturdays.

- Be respectful. Some teachers feel the need to establish their authority. In these cases, be understanding—and don't be the one who ends up in the principal's office. On the other hand, just as many teachers enjoy a good banter now and then, and they don't mind if you say you don't like their Bambi poster. But until you get a sense of what the teacher is like, be on your best behavior just in case.

- Answer questions. Teachers hate asking a question and looking at a class full of blank stares. When the teacher asks something and you can answer it, do. This will be your ticket into the "intelligent" group in the teacher's head, and it will keep you from being trapped in the purgatory of the blank stare.

- Suppress the urge to be a smart aleck or a class clown. If the temptation to make witty asides and outrageous comments is alluring, try to temper your temptation for the first few weeks. Teachers will want to make sure that you and the other students in your class know that high school is serious business. Your joking may make the teacher uncomfortable at first. Later in the year, after you get to know the teacher, you might feel comfortable saying stupid stuff that will make the class laugh— but it's a lot funnier if the teacher is laughing, too.

- Smile, nod, and look interested. For truly savvy students, this is a great tool. Even if he or she is mostly blind and forgets his or her miracle ear half the time, the teacher will definitely notice and appreciate your attention in class. Such attention may positively affect your grade, especially in classes where grading is somewhat subjective (which is in most classes). Even if you don't get extra credit for paying attention in class, you will definitely get more out of class time, and it will show on tests. For those with extraordinary acting skills, make it seem like all you want to do is understand. Nod a lot. For the rest of us, it helps if you are actually trying to understand.

6. HIGH SCHOOL CLASSES OFTEN HAVE A MIXTURE OF AGES, WHICH IS REALLY NOT A BIG DEAL.

One of the coolest things about high school is that you are not stuck with the same 20 kids for every class, as when you were in middle school or elementary school. Don't be intimidated when there's a junior or senior in your PE class or other electives. Don't worry, they probably won't even notice you. Just accept your current station and look forward to the day when you'll be an upperclassman.

If there's a senior in your algebra class, he will probably feel more uncomfortable than you because he will be the odd man out. For you, this may be a great opportunity to get to know an older student—and even if he is taking algebra for the fourth time, that doesn't mean he can't help you out with history or advice on driver's ed. Take advantage of classes that include a mixture of ages—they are one of the new opportunities that high school offers.

7. High school classes are harder—be realistic and go easy on yourself.

It will take some time to adjust and learn the ins and outs of your new classes. Don't stress out. Try to see your freshman year, though important, as only a small part of your high school career. Work hard, but don't kill yourself if you are not getting everything immediately. If you got straight A's in middle school, you might or might not be a straight-A student in high school. And if you don't get your best grades the first semester of freshman year, well, join the club: Almost everyone takes a little while to adjust. Be realistic about the expectations you set for yourself. Give it the old college try, as they say, but also give it time. Success will come; enjoy the ride.

At first, high school may seem so overwhelming with all new classes and a new environment that you may want to move to Timbuktu. The only thing we can say is that it gets easier. The combination of the new environment, new people, new status as the youngest, and the new course load can be daunting. But once the eternity of the first month or two passes, some of the scarier parts of high school disappear and even seem silly. You will get comfortable in school, you'll get to know your way around, you'll start knowing people, you'll be okay about being a freshman, and you'll be better able to deal with classes.

Basically, the point is, it gets easier. Blues Traveler sings a song called "Just Wait"—take John Popper's advice, it does get easier.

CHAPTER 4

New Expectations: Getting Accustomed to High School Life

I remember in eighth grade when the high school counselors came to talk to us about the joys of our soon-to-be ninth-grade lives. They preached about the new friends we were going to make and how much fun we were going to have. Like good salesmen, they promoted only the best side of their product. When I look back, after graduation, I'll miss dearly the people, the teachers, the spirit, and the dances. But what about the homework, the stress, the essays, and the late nights? I think not. Somehow the counselors forgot to mention those.

For the first week of ninth grade, high school was all I had hoped it would be. I didn't care if I was getting six hours of sleep; I had better things to do than sleep. There were new people to meet, old friends to see, and plenty of older girls to gawk at. I hit the first weekend feeling like a million bucks. The next Monday morning, however, hit me like a smack in the face. Classes were getting serious—no more tours of the new school. And,

> *boy, was I tired. I survived freshman year by taking each morning one at a time and trying not to think about the 719 more that lay ahead.*
>
> —ANDREW, MERCER ISLAND HIGH SCHOOL, MERCER ISLAND, WASHINGTON

The transition from middle school to high school is filled with all kinds of new expectations. Many students fear their first few weeks of high school, but with a few tips and a positive outlook, you can effortlessly glide through that first quarter. At first, your new high school may seem like a scary, confusing place, but once you get accustomed to high school life, you'll love it.

New classes and teachers often intimidate incoming freshmen, and many students find it hard to adjust to high school. The people around you just seem to demand more from you and have higher expectations of you. Don't worry, just stay calm. If you enter high school with an open, confident attitude, conquering these obstacles will be no problem. With a little bit of preparation, you can learn to succeed in difficult classes, work with your new teachers, and have a good time.

This chapter is filled with tips to help you handle and enjoy the new responsibilities that come with high school.

1. YOUR COUNSELOR EXPECTS YOU TO FIND HER, NOT VICE VERSA.

Many incoming students avoid visiting their counselors. As soon as you can, however, arrange a meeting with your counselor because this person may play a vital role in your high school success and college acceptance. Your counselor will help you prepare for upcoming tests, such as the SAT or ACT. He or she will also assist you in selecting and applying to colleges. Make that extra trip down to the counseling center, and get to know your counselor early on. The meeting will not only provide you with a whole bunch of helpful hints and tips, but it will also soften the transition into high school.

2. YOU ARE EXPECTED TO KNOW HOW TO MANAGE YOUR TIME.

The key to surviving high school is proper time management. (See Chapter 21, "Time Management.") Without a planned schedule, you will probably find yourself forgetting assignments you didn't even know you had. Most teenagers have sports, homework, and extracurricular activities every day. If you want to have time and sanity left over for your fun activities, you need to take care of schoolwork first. Otherwise, you'll end up playing soccer until 8 p.m., only to find out that you have no time left to finish your biology lab. What's more, teams usually won't let you play if you are failing more than one class.

Every student will have a different time-management technique that works for him or her. Many schools hand out assignment notebooks, where you can write down your homework assignments and schedule long-term projects. By using a notebook or a simple calendar, you will not only remember your homework, but you will also be able to look ahead and be ready when the due date for that big project comes along. If you can balance your schedule, you will use your time most efficiently and save time for extra activities.

No matter how busy your life was in middle school, it will get even more hectic in high school. If you find yourself with a few extra moments when you aren't practicing, studying, or thinking about school or extracurricular/social activities, use this time well. Take a bath, watch a TV program, walk the dog, whatever. Don't take this time for granted: Moments like this will be sanity-savers.

> *Slacking off in eighth grade left me grossly unprepared for high school. A year of procrastinating led to horrible study habits. It seemed like every night in my freshman year, I remembered all the assignments I had to do at about 9 p.m. As soon as I was going to start my homework, it seemed a TV show too good to miss came on. Whether it was* The Simpsons *or* Seinfeld *or something I didn't even want to watch, it all looked*

> *better than studying. About one-third of the way through my freshman year, a counselor came to talk to our class about time management. He told us to set aside at least two hours a night just for studying. This way you're guaranteed to do your homework because you have a set time and you are not just telling yourself, "Oh, I'll do it later."*
>
> —JOHN, MERCER ISLAND HIGH SCHOOL, MERCER ISLAND, WASHINGTON

3. PEOPLE EXPECT YOU TO KNOW THE ROPES.

Of course you are going to get lost a few times in the first week. Of course you are going to get confused about which period starts when. But everyone will expect you to adjust pretty quickly. This doesn't mean you won't get cut a little slack on the first few days, but as soon as the first week's over, you'll be expected to know the routine, the rules, and your way around campus. Make sure that you get your grounding during the first week; if you need help, ask a teacher or an upperclassman.

4. TEACHERS EXPECT YOU TO COMMUNICATE WITH THEM.

To succeed in your classes, you need to get to know your teachers. Teachers are there for a reason: to help you learn. Take advantage of this. Don't spend hours toiling over an algebra theorem you don't understand; ask your teacher for help whenever you need it, especially if you know you're going to be tested on something you don't understand. You might not have needed help in middle school—or maybe when you did need help, the teacher was always looking over your shoulder. That's not so in high school. Teachers are happy to help, but you have to ask for it.

Teachers have different methods and styles as well. If you want to get the grades, you need to cater to what they ask you to do. By communicating with them, you will not only gain a better understanding of what they expect, but you also will help them understand what you expect from them. Teachers are one of your most valuable tools for high school survival.

5. TEACHERS EXPECT YOU TO DEAL WITH HOMEWORK OVERLOAD. (AAAAH!)

After the first week of high school—which is usually more laid-back (although not in all cases)—you are going to receive a lot of homework. Be prepared to work for at least a few hours every weekday night. Try not to freak out about the homework load you get at first. Often, teachers try to intimidate you by giving you a lot of homework in the first quarter to show that you will not be able to slack off in their classes. As unfair and scary as it may seem, this will only prepare you for your future years. You will eventually learn to finish your homework in a quick, efficient, and acceptable manner (at least in theory—actual results may vary!). Once you get into the swing of things, homework will be less and less of an ordeal, and it will become more routine. After all, you have to plow through the bad to get to the good.

> *High school seemed to me to be the perfect time in my life. I mean, all you hear about from the beginning of middle school until your last day is that high school is a blast. Besides independence and being able to drive, there's also the parties, dances, football games—the whole American high school ideal. Little did I know that I would miss half the parties because of homework, or that I would leave the football game early to go study, or that I would use the car to drive to the library on Sunday morning. I mean, high school was a ton of fun, but it was much more demanding than I expected. There's a lot more responsibility because if you succeed in high school, you will be set up for success in college— and if you succeed in college, you can get a successful job. You get the point. High school was a wake-up call for me.*
>
> —SMITA, INTERNATIONAL HIGH SCHOOL, BELLEVUE, WASHINGTON

6. TEACHERS EXPECT YOU TO BE THERE—ON TIME.

In some classes, being tardy counts against your grade, and being tardy a lot kills your grade. You need to come to class on time every day. By not being present for the first part of class, you miss important information. Do whatever it takes to wake up on time. When traveling from class to class, try to avoid talking with friends for too long in the halls. Before you know it, you'll be walking into class 5 minutes late. Coming late to class makes it harder on both you and your teacher, who probably will feel the need to punish you and your tardiness as an example to the rest of the class.

7. TEACHERS EXPECT YOU TO PAY ATTENTION.

This one goes out to all you daydreamers out there. To understand what you are studying, the information must enter your brain through osmosis (or something like that). In layman's terms, you have to listen. If you don't pay attention in class, you are probably not going to understand your homework assignment. Unlike middle school, homework in high school is often tied to in-class lectures; it isn't something you can learn by yourself at home. Do all that it takes to remember what your teacher says in class. Take notes. Remember, you often can learn more from your teacher than you can from your book, and it's probably faster to listen in class than to try to figure it all out from the reading. Plus, the teacher will be watching you like a hawk, and you can bet that if you're the one who's always talking to the person in the next desk, or the one who falls asleep every day, you won't be remembered kindly when grading time comes.

8. TEACHERS EXPECT YOU TO TURN IN YOUR ASSIGNMENTS ON TIME.

Homework accounts for a big percentage of your grades in high school, and teachers expect you to finish all your homework on time. They aren't nearly as lenient as your middle school teachers were, which means you are going to have to keep an accurate record of upcoming due dates and deadlines. If you're the type who waits until the last minute or who frequently forgets important assignments, you are going to need to rethink your strategy. Many teachers in high school won't accept late homework.

I remember, in middle school, due dates on projects were ignored completely. Coming to school with an assignment two weeks overdue was a common occurrence. I spent three years in that type of atmosphere and grew accustomed to it; I wish that I hadn't. When I entered high school, everything changed. My first major project was assigned in English. The due date approached, and I hadn't started on it. The middle school mentality of asking for extensions hadn't left me. After class, the day before the assigned date, I asked the teacher if I could turn in the project a little late. Her response was classic: "Sure you can, but I'll just give you half the points." My jaw hit the floor. How was I expected to complete a project assigned three weeks ago overnight? I spent a sleepless night toiling over the project until it was finished. I learned the hard way: In high school, you have to get organized and turn in assignments on time.

—Anisha, Sammamish High School, Bellevue, Washington

9. Teachers expect you to participate in class.

For many teachers, participation is as important as homework in determining your grade. Most teachers in high school expect you to participate actively in class. Without observing some form of participation, your teachers cannot tell whether you understand the subject. If you are shy and don't really feel comfortable making spontaneous comments, then you might try writing down a few comments the night before so that you're sure to have something to contribute. Raise your hand in class or make relevant comments. By actively participating in group discussions, you will not only feel that you have contributed to the class, but you will also gain a better understanding of the subject at hand. Positive participation will do nothing but help you both learn and get better grades.

10. You should expect yourself to be rested and energized for the day.

Without sleep or breakfast, your attention span during your morning classes is likely to be approximately 3 to 5 minutes. This means you learn zilch, nada, nothing. Make sure that you at least grab a banana on your way to school. Try to get at least eight hours of sleep a night. You need to fuel your body to keep up with the numerous responsibilities of high school. (Check out Chapter 23, "Nutrition: Eating Right and Living Right in High School.")

When All Else Fails, Ask Someone

You will face many other new expectations in high school—we couldn't list them all here if we tried. Remember to ask for help if you have a question. For example, if you are unsure what a teacher means when he or she asks you to cite four sources in your essay, ask for clarification. The rest of the class will probably be grateful that you had the guts to speak up and say what everyone else was thinking. If you feel you are asking too many questions, ask a friend what he or she thinks. If your friend tells you that you are being a little annoying, tone it down and maybe save some of your questions for after class. In most cases, though, the best solution is to raise your hand and get your questions answered quickly.

As stressful as high school is, there is always time for fun. No one can survive by working all day long. Remember that although you face a ton of new expectations, there is no excuse for not taking a little time to call a friend, go to a movie, or perhaps hit around a tennis ball. The real world is still a few years off, so don't miss out on some of the best parts of still being in high school.

CHAPTER 5

Homework: A Necessary Evil

I was sick of algebra, sick of grammar, sick of French verbs. I had five months of school before summer vacation, and I didn't think I could possibly get through them. I wanted to scream and hit someone as much as I wanted to curl up and cry out of self-pity. I was just about to start throwing things at my brother when the phone rang for me. I was ready to whine and complain to whomever had made the mistake of calling me, when I was forced to forget a little of my own self-pity and just get over it. On the other line was my friend Alison, and she was crying. She said she was really stressed out and that she just couldn't finish her history paper. All of a sudden, I found myself in the position I had least expected to be. I had to tell her to calm down. (And I was the one who was ready to strangle anyone who tried to offer advice!) "Come on, Alison," I said. "Chill out. Just finish as much as you can. It's not a big deal—when you're 30 years old, you won't even remember this. It's not worth stressing about." And I began to listen to my own advice. Rather than just freaking out, I found ways to deal. The next week Alison and I were laughing over how stupid we sounded. "I

> *feel so dumb for going psycho over homework, of all things!" she said. "Don't tell anyone, okay?" Sorry, Alison.*
>
> —Merritt, Heritage High School, Littleton, Colorado

For some reason, the high school gods have ordered that homework be included in everyone's high school experience. What a way to ruin a totally fun time, eh? It's like making chocolate chip cookies and adding Brussels sprouts as a main ingredient. Well, homework may be a necessary evil in high school, but that doesn't mean that it can't be conquered. With a little strategizing, you can ensure that homework never gets the better of you. You can learn to minimize the time and effort that goes into homework and make sure that you always have the maximum amount of time to spend hanging out with friends, playing a sport, or just relaxing in front of the old TV.

Following is a list of tips designed to be your weapons against that necessary evil: homework.

1. Don't procrastinate.

Plan ahead. If you have a soccer game Thursday night, finish the assignment by Wednesday. Remember too that, while on Friday and Saturday it seems like you have ages before you need to do your homework, getting a head start will make your weekend much more relaxed and enjoyable—especially your Sundays. Try to get most of your homework done before Sunday night so that you can get to bed at a decent hour. Plus, what if you realize at the last minute that you need to go to the library for Cliff's Notes—er . . . I mean, the book you're reading in English? The library isn't open late Sunday night!

> *Last term I was given an independent study project to work on over about two months. I was supposed to read a book and write an essay on it. I didn't even start reading the book until a week before, and the whole*

> *week I was really tired. The night before it was due, I was too tired to do the assignment well. I wish I had thought ahead a little instead of thinking during all those months that I had plenty of time.*
>
> —PETER, HERITAGE HIGH SCHOOL, LITTLETON, COLORADO

2. TAKE DETAILED NOTES IN CLASS.

You may have a good memory, but unless you're Jane Austen's great-granddaughter, you probably won't remember all those grammar rules. And, hey, even Albert Einstein had to write down an algebra formula every once in a while—you probably should, too. Taking notes in class will help you remember things come test time and probably will lessen your homework load; for example, sometimes math teachers will do a problem on the board and then give you a very similar problem for homework. You'll wish you had taken notes when you are trying to reinvent the wheel.

3. BE SURE YOU UNDERSTAND THE ASSIGNMENT BEFORE YOU GET HOME.

If you don't understand the assignment in class, you won't understand it at home. Ask whatever questions you need and make sure that you understand the assignment. Chances are, you're not the only one who isn't sure what the teacher wants you to do. However, if you do happen to get home and find that you homework looks a lot like Sanskrit, don't just shove it back into your backpack. Look over your notes, and hopefully you'll figure it out. If you think you have some idea, give it a shot. A wrong try is better than having nothing to turn in at all. If, after reviewing your notes, you still have no idea how to do the assignment, then try calling a friend; if possible, see the teacher before class the next day.

4. KEEP TRACK OF YOUR ASSIGNMENTS BY WRITING THEM DOWN IN A NOTEBOOK.

With six or seven classes, even the most diligent students can forget an assignment or two. To keep everything straight—and to make sure that you won't forget any of your homework—keep track of your assignments by writing them down on a piece of paper in your folder or, even better, in an assignment notebook. Make a column where you can check off finished assignments. Checking off your assignments will give you a sense of accomplishment and also clearly show which assignments you still have to do. Also make a column where you will write how much time each assignment will take (be generous in your estimations) so that you can plan your evenings accordingly.

5. Use some of your free time at school to complete your homework.

If you finish all or most of your homework during study hall or a free period, you'll have less to do at home. Granted, it's hard to resist sitting in the cafeteria and chatting with friends, but try to strike a balance between socializing and finishing your work.

6. Make goals for yourself and give yourself incentives.

Set a goal like this: "If I can finish all my homework before Sunday, I will treat myself to a movie, ice cream at Baskin-Robbins, or perhaps just time to hang out with friends." Instead of just going out and buying yourself that new pair of shoes that you've been saving up for, use it as an incentive for getting all your homework in on time for a week. Goals help you concentrate better and give you an incentive to keep working when the TV is calling your name from the other room.

Little breaks can also help. Most people need a break after about an hour of studying. Tell yourself, "Once I finish this chapter in history, I'll go get a snack." Or, go shoot a few hoops. Or, make a quick gossipy phone call. Beware, though, of short breaks that end up lasting for a few hours. It's okay to shoot a few hoops for a break, but it's probably not okay to play a few games until 10 p.m. Calling your friend for a short break is perfectly fine, but sometimes gossiping can last for more than a few minutes. Use your judgment about which types of study breaks will be short and which ones will take longer.

7. Don't do homework while lying on your bed.

Sleep is one of homework's biggest enemies, especially if you are reading a textbook on something you're not particularly interested in or an old English novel using language from hundreds of years ago. Stay away from your bed. Study at your desk. Study at your computer. Study in the kitchen. Uncomfortable chairs can help you stay awake.

8. DON'T DO HOMEWORK ON THE PHONE (UNLESS YOU HAVE TO).

Working on the phone will take longer with the added gossip. It's not very efficient. Besides, it always seems like your brother or sister is yelling at you to get off *now*. Do your homework on your own, if you can, and save your phone time for socializing. Of course, if you need help or forget an assignment, calling a friend is usually a good bet.

9. FIND A QUIET PLACE TO WORK.

Everybody has a different style when it comes to studying. Go to a place where you won't get distracted—you'll finish sooner and do a better job. For some people, that might be an empty classroom after school, for some it might be their room at home, for others the public library—whatever you do, don't try to work somewhere where you will just end up wasting time.

10. USE YOUR PARENTS AND OLDER SIBLINGS FOR HELP, BUT STICK WITH THE TEACHER'S METHODS.

A parent or sibling can be a great proofreader on a research paper. Ask for help before you need it, and try to finish early enough so that your parent or sibling has enough time to do a good job (and so that you have enough time to make corrections). If they can spot a few typos or point out a flaw that you can fix, you may have moved yourself up from a B to an A. If a math problem is especially hard, sometimes sitting down with your dad or mom or big brother or sister can get you out of a rut. For example, your father might point out that you used a negative sign in an equation when you should have been using a positive sign. Sometimes other people can spot little things that you can't see because you're concentrating on a different part of the problem.

Even if you let your parents help you, though, you still should try to use the teacher's methods. Many things have changed since your parents were in school. You don't want your teacher looking at your homework and wondering why you are using formulas that haven't been used since the time of covered wagons.

11. DON'T DO HOMEWORK WHILE DOING SOMETHING ELSE.

Talking on the phone (as mentioned earlier) or watching TV make it much harder for you to concentrate. When your full attention is not on your work, you will take a lot longer and probably will not do as good of a job. Even music can sometimes be distracting; while it's tempting to put on your new techno CD, don't put on something that will have you dancing around the room. Instead, use these activities as incentives. If you can get your homework done first, you will be able to devote yourself completely to your favorite TV show later.

> *The other night I was sitting in the family room in my house, trying to read* A Christmas Carol, *take notes, and watch a cheesy made-for-TV movie called* Asteroid *all at once. Needless to say, I was less than successful. It took me three hours to read 10 pages!*
>
> *It's so hard to discipline yourself to stay in your room and get homework done, especially when the TV is beckoning from just a few yards away!*
>
> —GWIN, MULLEN HIGH SCHOOL, DENVER, COLORADO

12. COMPLETE ALL ASSIGNMENTS, EVEN IF THEY'RE GOING TO BE LATE.

Even if the teacher doesn't check the homework every day, the work will catch up with you. Try to turn in all your assignments on time— you're probably going to do them at some point anyway, so why wait? But even if an assignment is late, turn it in. Doing the work will not only help you on the test, but you will probably get some credit—and, if not, the teacher will appreciate your effort, which can affect your grade. Plus, if you're really lucky, when you turn in an assignment late the teacher won't even notice, or he will forget to mark it late in the grade book.

13. DON'T COPY OTHER PEOPLE'S HOMEWORK.

When you copy other people's homework, you get out of the work for the moment, but the assignment doesn't go away. When you are handed a test that looks like Swahili, you probably won't be too psyched about the homework assignment your pal let you copy. Not only will the teacher wonder why you have perfect homework and then fail tests, but the homework you copied may be completely wrong anyway. Plus, what happens if you are asked on a test to explain your thinking? You'll be up a creek—it's pretty tough to explain thinking that you haven't thunk!

Of course, we haven't even talked about what happens if you get caught: Most high school teachers and principals take copying homework and other kinds of cheating pretty seriously. Getting an F on those assignments might be the least of your problems.

14. IF THERE IS A GROUP ASSIGNMENT, DON'T ALWAYS HEAD FOR YOUR BEST BUDS. USE STRATEGIC PARTNER PLANNING.

While it's tempting to head straight to friends and turn the assignment into social hour, your grade will probably reflect your choice of partners. Your best friend might be great to chat with on the phone, and that football player might be the hottest guy in school, but before you choose a partner, you want to be sure that he or she is going to do an equal share of the work. Don't worry about offending good friends—just tell them that you don't want to be distracted while working. They'll respect that getting the grade is important to you. Choose a partner you can work well with and who will do an equal share of the work.

15. MAKE A COMMITMENT TO GIVE HOMEWORK PRIORITY OVER OTHER ACTIVITIES—AND SCHEDULE YOUR TIME ACCORDINGLY.

If you find that you're not even starting your homework until 10 p.m., then think back on your daily schedule: Was there any time you just sort of wasted that you could have used more profitably doing homework? Was there time during school that you spent talking to friends when you could have been finishing up assignments? Did you watch a few hours of TV? If not, then perhaps you are involved in too many activities. You may have to decide to eliminate one of them so that you have more time to devote to studying.

16. WORK AHEAD ON LONG-TERM PROJECTS.

If the teacher gives you more time for a project, the reason is probably that it is going to take you longer than one night. Don't leave that assignment until the night before: You're just creating stress for yourself. The teacher won't be very sympathetic if you go in for help the day it's due, either. Get started early. If it is a research paper, do your library research well ahead of time. Working ahead will just make your life easier.

17. LET THE TEACHER KNOW IN ADVANCE IF YOU NEED EXTRA TIME FOR AN ASSIGNMENT.

If you follow these tips and budget your time well, you should be able to turn in all your assignments on time. But if you know an assignment is going to be late, don't wait to give your excuse until the teacher is collecting the homework in class. Go in and speak to the teacher before class; in the case of a long-term assignment (such as a research paper), go in at least a day early, if possible. By talking with the teacher in advance, the worst that can happen is that you get the late grade you would have gotten anyway—you have nothing to lose! On the other hand, if you are sympathetic (and very lucky!), the teacher might appreciate your diligence and give you an extension.

> *Last semester in math class, the teacher came up to me one day and told me that I had six zeros in a row in her grade book. Of course, I knew that I was way behind, but I thought she hadn't noticed. So I just acted real surprised and asked her what I should do.*
>
> *She said that if I turned them all in the next day, she would give me half-credit. So, I had to stay up almost all night catching up. But I got it all done, and at least I got some credit instead of having all those zeros in the grade book.*
>
> *I learned two things: (1) Never assume that you are fooling the teacher; and (2) I never want to do six math lessons in one night again!*
>
> —JARED, HARWICH HIGH SCHOOL, HARWICH, MASSACHUSETTS

18. DON'T REINVENT THE WHEEL.

If you have hit a writer's block while tackling your big research paper or are trying hopelessly to read and understand Shakespeare, don't fret—some very smart people may have already done some of the dirty work for you. Unless your teacher instructs you otherwise, there is nothing wrong with reading supplemental materials, such as Cliff's Notes, which essentially try to explain your reading in more simple, concise terms. If it helps you understand what is going on, reading supplemental stuff can actually make a difficult read such as Shakespeare's *Hamlet* or *King Lear* more enjoyable. Of course, we are not advocating plagiarizing, which involves taking credit for other people's work, or reading only the Cliff's Notes instead of the real thing. But realize that the best research papers often explain the ideas of others and attempt to improve on those ideas with new ones based on personal experiences. By the way, if you think your teachers have not read the Cliff's Notes, think again: There's about a 100 percent chance they have, and a better than likely chance that you'll get caught if you plagiarize. You can use supplemental materials, but don't copy them!

19. GET TO SLEEP AT A DECENT HOUR.

If you have a ton of homework on a certain night, give yourself an assigned bedtime—maybe 11 p.m. Divide the time you have left into equal time slots for each subject; if you're starting at 7 p.m. and you have homework in math, English, science, and French, then give yourself an hour for each. If you're not done at the end of that hour with one subject, move on anyway; if you finish another subject early, go back to the one you need more time on. This way, you don't fall back in all your classes just because you're struggling with the work in one. Plus, spending a long time at one subject can result in major brain-frying. It's much easier to alternate between subjects.

20. DON'T LET HOMEWORK GET YOU DOWN.

Homework can be just a small part of school that you do as part of your daily ritual, or it can be something that hangs over your head and ruins your weekend. Don't let it rule your life by stressing you out. Sure, when you're sick or you miss a day or two of school, you may have to spend a couple late nights making up assignments, but you're just wasting time by worrying. If you make homework part of a daily ritual and dedicate a small portion of your day to finishing it, you'll find that it isn't really that bad—and that it's certainly not worth stressing out.

> *Last year, I was completely overwhelmed with the workload I was getting from my science class. It became a big deal, and I always felt like I was behind, even though I'd be up at all hours working on homework. Finally, I realized that I was the only one freaking out about science. I started just working more in class and not worrying if everything wasn't exactly how the teacher asked. I realized I'd been creating a lot of stress for myself, and the only reason homework had been a big deal was because I made it one.*
>
> —DORIE, KENT SCHOOL, DENVER, COLORADO

FINISHING UP . . .

Basically, the best thing that you can do with homework in high school is to make it take up the least amount of time and cause you the least amount of worry possible. If you approach your homework the right way and take these tips to heart, you can make sure that homework is not the most memorable part of your high school experience.

CHAPTER 6

Essay Writing: Dirty Work, but We All Have to Do It

> *I can never understand those people who can crank out essays as fast as their hands can type. I'm one of those people who has to really sit down and think before I even start typing—and even then, it often takes me hours to get my thoughts down on paper. A big time-saver is if you do the thinking before you're actually sitting in front of the screen. That way, you can sit down and know what your main ideas are. Also, if you're really having trouble, try just jotting down your ideas—even if they sound dumb—and see if any of them can get you started.*
>
> —PETER, HERITAGE HIGH SCHOOL, LITTLETON, COLORADO

The thought of writing essays, one of the most frequent high school assignments, sends most freshmen into a state of panic. However, as the pile of completed essays stacks up, the process only gets easier. It's true that the best way to get good at essay writing is just to do a whole lot of essays, and we're sure that your teachers will make sure that you do. But we hope that the following advice will make things a little bit easier. We're all about making your life a little easier and less stressful, and these tips can help you start down the path of good essay writing with as little pain as possible.

1. **FIND THE RIGHT ENVIRONMENT. ARE YOU COMFY ENOUGH? ARE YOU TOO COMFY?**

The first step involves learning more about yourself and the conditions that affect your ability to work. Are you someone who requires absolute silence, bright lights, and a clear desk? Or are you more comfortable sprawled out on your bedroom floor with your favorite CD playing in the background? Factors such as music and light affect your comfort level. In some cases, music stimulates one's thoughts and helps to get ideas flowing. However, more frequently, music (especially music with words) is a distraction that disrupts your train of thought. Experiment with these factors to find an environment that suits your individual needs.

> *The afternoon before an essay was due, I had the opportunity to hang out at a pool with a bunch of friends. I promised myself I would get it done there; after a few hours of procrastinating, I finally got out of the water and began to write. With the music blasting, kids screaming, and the smell of barbecued hamburgers in the air, I had a hard time getting started. Frequent distractions made the process drudge on. Anxious to return to my group of friends, I wrote as quickly as possible, not really thinking about what I was saying. When I finished my conclusion, I didn't even read over my paper. I just shoved it in my bag, assuring myself that it was a good paper. Apparently, my teacher did not feel the same way when he returned my corrected essay to me.*
>
> —DIANA, MERCER ISLAND HS, MERCER ISLAND, WASHINGTON

2. **GETTING STARTED: FIND A THESIS STATEMENT.**

Your thesis statement is the single most important sentence in your essay. It embodies your entire argument; it is the focus of your whole paper. But, hey, no pressure. Just sit back, think about what you want to say, and make sure to heed the following tips.

- A thesis sentence must be an opinion, which means that it must be debatable. The purpose of your essay is to prove your thesis statement. If your thesis statement is "*Star Wars* was better than any of the prequels or sequels because it was first, was superbly written, and had the best characters," then the rest of your essay must be dedicated to proving the points of that thesis. Of course, this thesis is a debatable one for those who preferred *The Empire Strikes Back, Return of the Jedi,* and *The Phantom Menace.* Unfortunately, there is no magic formula for writing it. To produce a clear and concise statement, much rewording and reworking is often necessary.

- If a thesis statement does not come immediately to mind, you might try brainstorming on a blank piece of paper. What are the things that you want to talk about? Write down each idea as it comes to you. Maybe look back through the book or the history chapter that you have to write about, and see if anything new jumps out at you. After you're done writing down all your ideas, look through your list and try to find something that a lot of them have in common. Do several of your ideas have to do with the same character in a book? Are there a bunch of examples of how the Cold War affected America? Try to group your ideas, and then think of a way to summarize what they all say in one sentence. If you can summarize all your ideas in a single sentence, you have a thesis.

- Don't start writing your paper until you have a thesis or a rough idea of your thesis statement. If you do jump right in, you may likely end up with a disjointed jumble of facts, not an essay.

Have you ever started writing an essay by analyzing the topic first? I used to sit in front of my computer typing random pieces of analysis until a thesis came to me. One night, loaded with homework, I decided to

> *write my essay as fast as possible to escape pulling yet another all-nighter. So, I went through my analysis, edited it, and put it into formatted paragraphs. The next morning, during a peer edit session, my editor turned to me and said, "Um, Sunny, like, do you have a thesis statement?" I felt so stupid! I had forgotten to write a thesis! Ever since, my thesis has been the first thing I type.*
>
> —SUNNY, MERCER ISLAND HIGH SCHOOL, MERCER ISLAND, WASHINGTON

Here is an example of a strong thesis statement relating to the book *Lord of the Flies:* "Jack's authoritative attitude, Ralph's democratic nature, and Piggy's intellect make each boy suitable for leadership." This thesis statement consists of three main parts: Jack's authoritative attitude, Ralph's democratic nature, and Piggy's intellect. A thesis with three parts enables you to follow the general five-paragraph essay format, which is described next.

3. LEARN AND USE THE WORLD-FAMOUS FIVE-PARAGRAPH ESSAY FORMAT.

The five-paragraph essay begins with an introductory paragraph that introduces the topic, provides background information, and includes your thesis statement. The first sentence of the first paragraph is *not* your thesis statement; rather, the first sentence is more general, such as "A recent poll of critics found that *The Phantom Menace* was the best *Star Wars* movie." Several more introductory sentences may follow. Your thesis statement is the *last* sentence in the first paragraph, and it leads the way for the body of your essay.

The second paragraph is known as the first body paragraph. It is here that you prove your first point. Using the previous thesis statement about *Lord of the Flies*, the first body paragraph would focus on Jack's authoritative attitude. The first paragraph in the *Star Wars* essay would discuss the importance of *Star Wars* as the first movie. Following the first body paragraph are the second and third body paragraphs, in which the remaining two arguments are explored.

Each body paragraph should begin with a topic sentence that works like a thesis statement for that individual paragraph. For example, the first sentence of the first body paragraph in the *Star Wars* essay might be: "*Star Wars* was the first, and therefore the best, because first installments of series are the most difficult to write, produce, and direct." The rest of that paragraph would prove those three points.

Finally, paragraph five, the conclusion, sums up the entire essay and draws all the big ideas together. The first sentence of the conclusion paragraph should restate your thesis using different words. A good thesaurus is very handy for restating your thesis in the concluding paragraph. The final sentences of the conclusion should be more general. For example, in the *Star Wars* essay, you might talk about how the upcoming *Star Wars* movies may lead critics to rethink which one is the best of the series.

Even though some teachers may not admit it, most love the five-paragraph essay format: It makes their job easier because it forces you to write clearly and with purpose. Some teachers, especially in later years, may allow you to employ more flexible formats. But don't underestimate the 5-paragraph essay: It is suitable for almost every long essay you write in high school. You can use the general layout of a five-paragraph essay for a 5-page paper, a 10-page paper, or even a 20-page paper. When in doubt, stick to this format.

> *I think my dad summed it up best when he quoted the old adage about essays: First you tell 'em what you're going to tell 'em, then you tell 'em, and then you tell 'em what you told 'em.*
>
> —Peter, Heritage High School, Littleton, Colorado

4. Map out and outline your essay first.

Just as most people consult a map before taking a long car trip, it is wise to map out your key ideas before taking your long, essay-writing journey. Try to obtain a general sense of the direction your essay is headed. (This can also get you rolling if you're having a severe case of writer's block.)

One technique is to write the thesis in the middle of a blank sheet of paper and then jot down various ideas that stem from the thesis statement. Known as mind-mapping, this method helps you explore the various paths your essay can follow. By listing random thoughts pertaining to your paper, your essay also will consist of more in-depth and unique ideas. Moreover, this format helps to eliminate repetition in your writing.

A second technique, know as outlining, also helps spur new and creative thoughts. However, this technique is used more as an organizational tool. Outlining each paragraph help you to arrange your thoughts. By writing down your main point and then listing all the supporting evidence below, you are setting up guidelines that will simplify the writing process.

Both mind-mapping and outlining are good tools for beginner and more advanced essay writers. You can use both at the same time if you want.

5. FIGURE OUT WHAT'S IMPORTANT AND WHY.

When analyzing your essay, always try to grasp the big picture. To get out of a rut, ask yourself questions, such as "Why is this important?" and "What does this show?" These questions often lead to expanded ideas that help you connect specific examples to the thesis statement.

6. MAKE LOGICAL TRANSITIONS.

As you move from one point to the next, employ transitional statements to help the reader follow your thought process. Transitional phrases help your essay flow smoothly from one idea to the next. Common transition words or phrases include: *in addition to, furthermore, moreover, similarly, however,* and *on the contrary.* These phrases enable the reader to make the connection from past ideas to upcoming ones. They are usually used within paragraphs, although sometimes they can be placed at the beginning of a new paragraph.

7. FOCUS ON THE DETAILS.

Once you have the basic format down, you can start to develop your own tone or personality. In establishing your writing voice, several writing laws will help make your sentences stronger and more concise:

- The first rule is definitely the most challenging: no linking (or passive) verbs. Linking verbs are less forceful than action verbs, so use strong verbs. Take a look at this example of a sentence with linking verbs, followed by one with action verbs: "The stereo *was* repaired after the missing part arrived." A stronger way to say this is: "The technician *repaired* the stereo after the missing part arrived." In good writing, someone must be carrying out an action. A good way to identify linking verbs and passive voice in your writing is to look for a version of the verb *to be* followed by another verb in the past tense. For example, in the passive sentence "I was shown the door," the word *was* is a past-tense version of *to be* and *shown* is the past tense of *to show*. Instead, you should try to write a stronger, active sentence, such as "She showed me the door."

- A second hint is to keep your writing in the present tense. Unless you're writing about a historical event, present tense is more effective because it draws the reader closer to the issue. What you say in the present tense is true now, whereas if you talk in the past tense it sounds like what you're saying may have been true some time ago.

- Whichever tense you choose, make sure that you remain consistent throughout your essay.

- Watch out for clichés. This technique weakens even the strongest essays. A cliché is an overused expression, such as "it is raining cats and dogs." Clichés are uninteresting and become trite through overuse; they also suggest a lack of imagination. For example, you would not want to say something like, "When Romeo climbed the balcony, he proved to Juliet that actions speak louder than words." Besides the fact that this sentence is a relatively silly analysis, the cliché at the end of the sentence is likely to give any English teacher nightmares. Please ignore all the clichés in this book—to use a cliché, do as we say, not as we do.

- Lastly, an extended vocabulary is always impressive, so get to know your thesaurus. (You probably don't even need to have a thesaurus in book form; most word-processing programs have one under the Tools bar.) Finding synonyms for commonly used words adds variety and makes your paper more interesting. However, it is important not to get "thesaurus-happy." Too many dazzling words will undoubtedly confuse the reader. Sometimes thesauruses don't give you words with the *exact* meaning that you're looking for, either; if you overuse them, you might find yourself saying things that you don't really mean.

8. USE YOUR OWN WORK.

Cheating is not for the faint of heart. Some teachers treat cheating so severely that they require students to sign no-cheating contracts at the beginning of the year. No matter what the consequence (and the consequence in some schools is expulsion), cheating is never worth it. Eventually, you will probably get caught—and even if you don't, why take the chance? Getting a good grade on a paper you copied does not feel half as good as a good grade on one that you did yourself.

Never give someone else a paper that you have written. This is a bad idea! When I was in tenth-grade English, I had a teacher who I did not get along with. Every time I got a paper back, she had marked off points but never seemed able to tell me why. I'm sure we've all had a teacher like this at some point. I decided that I would just gut out the year and simply continue to try my hardest. One day, a friend of mine who was in college came to me and said, "You've got to help me! I forgot to read To Kill A Mockingbird, *and the paper is due tomorrow!" Since I had just read the book and turned in the paper, I readily changed the name in the heading to that of my friend, printed it out, and gave it to her to turn in to her college professor. I thought that was the kind of thing to do for a friend. And anyway, who was I hurting? Well, I soon found out. When the grades got back, I was shocked! I received a*

> *D-, while my college friend had gotten a B+. And on the same paper! Who could I tell? So, if for no other reason, don't share your papers because you may just end up feeling like an idiot when the grades return.*
>
> —RACHEL, ANNAPOLIS, MARYLAND

If you're having trouble pounding out an essay, it's perfectly okay to call a classmate to ask if he or she can help you sort out your ideas, but resist the temptation to copy from a friend. Ask your parents or a friend to help you proofread a paper, but don't let them write it for you. Also, if you think that you can get away with copying from a book or Cliff's Notes, think again. Your teacher probably has read Cliff's Notes and supporting materials. In many cases, that's how they prepare for class. The truth is that study aids can help you get better grades if used appropriately; just don't copy directly from them.

9. GIVE YOURSELF ENOUGH TIME.

One of the best ways to make sure that you do well on your essays in high school is to give yourself enough time to get them done. Until you get into the swing of things, it may take you several nights to write an essay. Your writing won't be as good when you have a 10-page paper to write and the due date is the next morning. Plan ahead to give yourself enough time. For longer papers, reserve a few days for research or outlining and one or two for writing.

> *Never write an essay after 3 a.m.! Unfortunately, I learned this important strategy through experience. I began writing my essay at 2:30 a.m. the night before the paper was due. At the time, I was extremely proud of my historical examples and quotes I had gathered. However, after submitting my essay, I began to worry about what I had actually written. Several days later, when my teacher handed back the corrected essays, mine came back with red ink all over it. Not only had*

> *I misspelled almost every other word, but I had incorporated sentences like, "McCarthyism, a direct result of purple dogs and macaroni . . . " into every quote. Needless to say, I did not get a very good grade on that essay.*
>
> —LAURA, MERCER ISLAND HS, MERCER ISLAND, WASHINGTON

10. SPELL-CHECK AND PROOFREAD.

With today's word-processing programs, spell-checking and grammar-checking is as simple as a few button clicks. Do it! Grammar-checking on the computer is still not state-of-the-art, but it catches some mistakes. After you have proofread an important paper, you might ask a parent or friend to proofread your paper as well. A third person can find mistakes that you don't see as the author. Eliminating silly mistakes—especially spelling mistakes—is the best way to bump up your grade from a C to a B, or from a B to an A.

YES YOU CAN!

By now, you're surely ready and excited to write your first essay! Well, even if that's not the case, don't forget these 10 tips. Good luck on your next big essay!

CHAPTER 7

Tests: A Nightmare, True or False?

> *The best piece of advice that I can give about tests in general is to definitely know what is going to be on the test, and to make sure that you're confident in these areas—it's guaranteed that the one thing you didn't study is going to be on the test. Second, concentrate on the test and don't risk it all by cheating. Lastly, once you've taken the test, don't keep freaking out. Once you've turned it in, it's over; you may as well concentrate your energies on something productive.*
>
> —LYNN, KENT DENVER HIGH SCHOOL, DENVER, COLORADO

You wake up and glance at the clock on your bedside table. With a jolt, you realize you have overslept your alarm, and that you are already late for school. You cringe as you remember that you had been planning to get up early to study before your first-hour economics test. Rushing out of the house, you grab something to eat and fly at break-neck speed toward campus. After racing up two flights of stairs, you burst into your classroom, only to realize your shoes don't match, you are still wearing the T-shirt you slept in, you have an orange juice mustache, and there is a piece of Pop Tart stuck in your hair. The entire class that was previously engrossed in a 12-page test bursts out laughing. Sound like a nightmare on test-taking day?

The following is a list of suggestions that should help you avoid such calamities and help you succeed as a test-taker in high school. We should say up front that none of these tips will help you with getting Pop Tart out of your hair. After reading the tips, though, we hope that this particular situation becomes your biggest test-taking problem.

PREPARING FOR TESTS

1. KEEP UP DAILY.

Take notes in class every day. Teachers tend to address in class most of the material that will appear on their tests. Notes, therefore, are necessary not only in helping you learn the material, but also in helping you review when the test is approaching.

If possible, review your notes nightly or weekly. On some nights or weeks, such review will be impossible if your workload in other classes is overbearing and you have kick-boxing class or other extracurricular activities. However, this type of constant reviewing is valuable because it further engrains the concepts in your mind.

Finally, it is important that you do all the assigned reading in a timely fashion. Keeping up in this manner is in itself a way of studying for a test. In addition, teachers often address the previous night's reading in class. To benefit from the teacher's lecture, therefore, you should have a basis of knowledge on the topic, which most often can be attained only from the assigned reading.

2. PREDICT WHAT TYPE OF TEST IT WILL BE.

Although predicting tests is difficult at the beginning of the year—mostly because you are not yet familiar with the teacher's techniques—it is extremely useful. Consider, for instance, his or her teaching style. Is he detail or concept oriented? Does she tend to give multiple-choice or essay tests? By predicting the form of the test, it is easier to prepare for it.

Listening closely to what the test will cover also might help you predict the type of test; if nothing else, this will ensure that you study the right information the night before a test.

> *Once I had a lapse of concentration during my French class, but I came out of school remembering that I had a test in French the next day. I studied Chapter 3 for several hours and felt that I had it mastered. But when I got to class the next day, I realized that the test was on Chapter 4. Although I nearly failed the test, I sure had Chapter 3 down, and I learned to listen closely to the teacher's explanations.*
>
> —MAGGIE, CHERRY CREEK HIGH SCHOOL, ENGLEWOOD, COLORADO

3. WHEN STUDYING, TRY TO PRETEND YOU ARE THE TEACHER.

Predict the questions that will be on the test when you are reviewing for it. What concepts has the teacher emphasized? How does this unit relate to the course as a whole? It is often useful to work with a classmate when trying to predict questions because you can combine your ideas. Be careful, however, not to make such a work session a social get-together. This is not a good time to paint your nails or start a pick-up street hockey game.

If you have the time, it is sometimes useful to design a practice test. While studying, pay special attention to the teacher's main points from the day before the test. These points are often included in the test because a teacher often writes the test several days before it is given. Usually, teachers will not hide the ball. They often will tell you what will be on the test to see if you are listening. Your job is to focus on those materials.

4. MAKE A STUDY SHEET OR AN OUTLINE.

These study aids do not take much time to create and are useful in organizing information. In addition, they make you feel less overwhelmed. The study sheet and outline should include information from your textbook, any additional reading, the notes from class, and information that was included in any quizzes given since the last test. On a math or science test, some sample problems might be useful on a study sheet.

5. ORGANIZE YOUR STUDY TIME IN SUCH A WAY THAT YOU PACE YOURSELF.

If possible, don't cram the night before the test. You'll retain the information best if you've been working with it over a long period of time. In addition, cramming is stressful.

One or two of your friends may be able to get A's by cramming for a test the night before, but most students can't succeed like that. Don't let a friend who can pull all-nighters and still get A's determine how you study for a test.

6. TRY TO GET A GOOD NIGHT'S SLEEP THE NIGHT BEFORE THE TEST.

Rest helps your mind to be alert and often eliminates some of the careless mistakes made on tests. True, you will often have a lot of studying to do the night before a big test, but it is usually more useful to get some extra sleep than to study late into the night. Who wants bags under the eyes anyway?

7. BEFORE A BIG TEST, TRY TO REMEMBER TO EAT A GOOD BREAKFAST OR LUNCH.

Although eating too much food might make you feel groggy (we all know what it's like to have a food coma in the period after lunch!), being hungry during test day is detrimental to your performance. You do not want to be focused on cupcakes when you should be grinding out algebraic formulas.

8. IMMEDIATELY BEFORE THE TEST, DO NOT TALK TO OTHER STUDENTS ABOUT IT.

This kind of conversation often makes you nervous. The last thing you want to hear from a classmate is that he or she studied for 5 hours the night before and feels completely prepared. If somebody says this to you, ignore that person and make plans to torture him or her later.

9. MAKE SURE YOU HAVE THE SUPPLIES YOU NEED.

To avoid added stress at the beginning of the test, come prepared with a watch, a pen or pencil, paper, and a calculator, if appropriate. Having these items with you might save you several minutes at the beginning of the exam.

10. Try to be on time to the test.

Punctuality eliminates some of the stress likely to occur on test-taking day. If you arrive on time to class, you will not miss any last-minute tips from the teacher and will have time to collect yourself before you start the test.

11. On test day, it may even help to wear comfortable clothes.

You do not want to be worried about your clothes or feel uncomfortable during a test. A comfortable pair of jeans should do the trick: You don't need to look particularly good to do well on a test.

> *It was the day before Halloween, and we were allowed to wear our costumes to school. I had to take a long U.S. history test in a large, frilly costume. Being in a school where a uniform is worn every day, it hadn't occurred to me that my attire could affect my test-taking experience. I was wearing a tight 1870s ball gown with long, lacy sleeves, a snug waist, and a long train that made it almost impossible for me to sit in my desk. It was my worst test-taking experience ever: It was hard to write and even harder to concentrate. From then on, I've dressed appropriately for tests.*
>
> —Jamie, The Hockaday School, Dallas, Texas

12. If possible, review just before the test.

Although cramming a lot of information into your mind just before you take a test is not a good idea, reviewing your notes or your study sheet the morning of a test is often beneficial. You will tend to forget things as time goes on, so studying the most important information the morning of a test is often useful.

TIPS FOR TEST DAY

1. AVOID TEST ANXIETY.

Many students get nervous when tests are handed out. Actually, a small adrenaline rush before an important test is beneficial in stimulating your concentration. However, to avoid stressing out at the beginning of a test, remember that you are prepared and then relax. You might even try taking a few deep breaths.

2. FIND A COMFORTABLE TEST SETTING.

You do not want to have to worry about a neighbor who is loud, who overdosed on perfume, or who has wandering eyes. If anything about someone who sits by you is distracting, you might want to try *quietly* asking the teacher if you can move. If this is not possible, block the distraction from your mind by plugging your ears or focusing on the question at hand.

3. LISTEN CAREFULLY TO WHAT THE TEACHER SAYS JUST BEFORE THE TEST.

Often a teacher will clarify parts of the test or give you last-minute advice for the exam. Although you may be nervous, do your best to listen.

4. ONCE YOU GET THE TEST, WRITE DOWN ANY KEY FACTS, FORMULAS, OR CHARTS IN THE MARGIN.

In writing such notes to yourself, you will ensure that you do not forget them, and you will have them available for easy access. On a chemistry test, for example, it is helpful to write down the formulas from the unit in the margin of the test.

5. SCAN THE TEST BEFORE YOU START.

Take note of the point value of each part of the test. You might want to start with the section that will award the most points to ensure that you have time to complete it. In addition, highlighting key words of instruction, such as *compare* or *define*, may help direct you toward the correct answer. It is also to your advantage to do the part that is easiest for you first: This method guarantees you those points.

6. STAY FOCUSED ON THE TASK AT HAND.

Forget about the beautiful day outside, the band practicing two floors above your classroom, and what you are going to do on Friday night. Even though a lot may have happened so far in the school day and there might be audible distractions in the classroom, it is critical to stay focused. Force yourself to concentrate on the problems if you find your mind wandering.

7. FOR EACH QUESTION, READ THE DIRECTIONS CAREFULLY.

Reading the directions on tests is crucial because some of the instructions may give you critical information on how to complete the test. Failing to read them would be like making a cake without reading the recipe.

> *Once, on a math test, the first page was full of instructions. Since the test was timed, and since I thought the instructions would be fairly straight-forward, I just went ahead and started to work. I spent almost all my time on problem five, so I didn't finish the test. It wasn't until my test was returned that I realized my mistake. Amidst the directions, in bold print, the teacher had stated that problem five was only to be done by the students in another class who had gotten further into the chapter. I learned my lesson that reading the directions makes a difference.*
>
> —CHRISTINE, THE HOCKADAY SCHOOL, DALLAS, TEXAS

8. IN READING EACH QUESTION, LOOK FOR QUALIFYING WORDS.

Words such as *all, none, always, never, often, rarely, many,* and *seldom* are important to note because they determine the direction in which the question is going. Imagine a true-or-false question such as, "In the 1920s, all people drove automobiles, the new symbol of wealth in America. " If you were asked to mark if this was true or false, it would be critical for you to have seen the word *all.* It is obvious, once this word is considered, that not all people drove cars. Overlooking the word *all* would have been a disaster. As a general rule, most true-or-false questions that use such words as *all, always, none,* or *never* are false. This makes sense because very few things are absolute.

9. On multiple-choice tests, eliminate answers to help find the correct one, and read all answer choices.

If a multiple-choice question has five answer choices, eliminating one or two right away helps you to focus on finding the correct answer. Reading all the choices for answers is critical because the last answer choice might be "all of the above." Don't just read the first answer and assume that you can move on to the next question.

10. On fill-in-the-blank tests, use the clues to your advantage.

If the word *a* precedes the blank, the word missing cannot start with a vowel (if it did, it would have to be *an* instead of *a*). Also, seek help from the context of the sentence if you are having trouble determining the best word for the blank. For example, if the sentence with the missing word is, "Guam is a _____ for America," the answer could not be "island," but could be "fueling station."

11. On matching tests with multiple answers, do the questions you know first.

By crossing out the choices that you know, matching the other words becomes easier. Think of it like doing a crossword puzzle.

12. On essay tests, start with an outline and thesis, use transition words and key phrases, be concise, and save time to write a conclusion.

Jotting down some of your thoughts before diving into an essay during a test is useful. This helps you to organize your thoughts and often helps remind you to include all logical points. Try to come up with a quick-and-dirty thesis, a succinct statement that pulls your whole essay together. (See Chapter 6, "Essay Writing: Dirty Work, but We All Have to Do It," for tips on thesis statements and essays in general.) Put the thesis in the very first paragraph; in a test where time is short, your thesis sentence may be your entire first paragraph. In addition, use transition words to help the essay flow. Throwing in some catch phrases—little sayings or words that your teacher likes to use in class—

is a sure way to get some extra points. Also, try to make your writing concise. After reading the essays of all the students in a class, a teacher appreciates essays that come to the point. Don't skimp on information, but try not to write a tome. Finally, try to save time to write a conclusion—this will make your writing seem more complete.

13. Lɪᴠᴇ ғᴏʀ ᴘᴀʀᴛɪᴀʟ ᴄʀᴇᴅɪᴛ.

Always write *something* down. Even if you do not know the answer to a question, it is usually a good idea to guess. If you only remember part of a formula, write down that part. If you only remember two reasons when the teacher wants three, write down the two reasons; make up a third. Teachers are usually good about partial credit because they like to see effort. Don't miss out on opportunities to get free points—you will get better at guessing with time.

14. Pᴀᴄᴇ ʏᴏᴜʀsᴇʟғ.

How often do you find yourself staring blankly at the clock in the middle of an important test? Instead, look into how long the class period is and how long you will have to finish the exam. Some exams are created to keep you moving and press you for time. On other tests, the emphasis lies elsewhere, and the teacher will allow you to work on the test after class or the next day. Some people even like to look through the test before they start any of the problems and set time limits for themselves on each section.

15. Dᴏɴ'ᴛ ᴘᴀɴɪᴄ ɪғ ʏᴏᴜ ᴀʀᴇ ʀᴜɴɴɪɴɢ ᴏᴜᴛ ᴏғ ᴛɪᴍᴇ.

Rushing through the last page of an important test will probably cause you to lose points. Instead of frantically trying to think of the answer while chewing on your eraser, keep working at the pace that is right for you. If you are writing an essay, write down your outline of the next points you were planning to make. If you have no more time to work on the test, at least your teacher will have an idea of where you were going with the essay. Often such an outline will get you partial credit.

16. Dᴏɴ'ᴛ ʙᴇ ғʟᴜsᴛᴇʀᴇᴅ ʙʏ ᴏᴛʜᴇʀ sᴛᴜᴅᴇɴᴛs ᴛᴜʀɴɪɴɢ ɪɴ ᴛʜᴇ ᴛᴇsᴛ ᴇᴀʀʟʏ.

Keep your own pace: It is usually a good idea to use all the time available to finish a test. Naturally, other students finishing before you is going to be distracting, but that should not influence your pace or concentration. Don't give yourself excuses for doing poorly; just focus on the job at hand.

17. Proofread your work if you have time.

The last thing you want to do is skip an entire page of a test. Look over your work, check any math problems for careless errors, and make sure that essays are logical. By proofreading, you may even find a misspelled word or a missing negative sign.

18. Finish any remaining problems.

If you have skipped ahead, use any extra time to go back and complete remaining problems. If you cannot answer the questions completely, remember to go for partial credit and write something—anything—down on your test. For multiple-choice questions, eliminate answers that you know are wrong and then make your best guess.

After the Test . . .

1. Relax until the test is returned.

There's no use fretting about a test once it has been completed. You can't change the way you did until you get it back, so worrying about your performance is useless. Also, badgering your teacher for results is not a good idea. Would you like people constantly asking you if your homework was finished?

Don't talk about the test with other students unless you know they want to discuss the test. Some students don't like talking about past exams and will find your questions and worrying annoying. If you did your best, take solace and move on to the next class.

2. Read the teacher's comments thoroughly.

When you see comments on tests, the teacher has put time into trying to help you. In reading over the comments, learn from your mistakes: Reading through the comments may help you on future tests.

> *Recently, I had a French teacher who gave us weekly quizzes with extra credit points possible. She gave an extra credit question one week, returned the quiz, and then gave the same extra credit question on the next two quizzes. She really wanted us to learn that word, and she hoped we would have learned from missing the extra credit points the first time.*
>
> —STEPHANIE, CHERRY CREEK HIGH SCHOOL, ENGLEWOOD, COLORADO

3. ASK YOUR TEACHER FOR HELP IF HIS OR HER COMMENTS DO NOT MAKE SENSE TO YOU.

Talking to your teacher about your mistakes will help you get the ideas straight and may help on future tests. Don't spend hours trying to figure out an answer. If you don't understand something, ask your teacher and use the extra time to watch TV or play some ball.

4. USE YOUR TESTS AS OUTLINES TO STUDY FOR FINALS.

Tests cover what the teacher thinks is important from specific units and are invaluable in studying for finals.

WRAPPING UP

Although some students think tests are the low point of high school, they do not have to be so painful. Remember the previous tips, and don't take any single test too seriously; you have more important tests in front of you. If you can, keep a positive attitude, too: Students who are positive tend to be more successful on tests and in high school in general.

CHAPTER 8

Teachers: Friends or Foes?

I went into my ninth-grade year expecting a big workload, and consequently labeling my teachers as the adversary. I was confused and tired when I walked into English class, my head still reeling from the history curriculum my teacher had just told us about. The first thing my teacher did was pass around a tea bag. She said, "I was getting my cup of tea this morning, and I found this tea bag. The funny thing is, it doesn't have any tea in it. It is empty, even though it smells like tea and even though it looks the same as all the other tea bags. I want you to write something, using this as a metaphor." Our class really got into it and came up with a ton of really cool ideas. The teacher said that tea bags are supposedly good luck, so she hung it above her desk. After we had all survived that first day, we built an even better relationship with the teacher, and we learned a lot. And every day when I was feeling particularly stressed or angry or sad, I would go sit under the tea bag and talk to her. She was definitely a friend as well as a teacher.

—NATALIE, EAST HIGH SCHOOL, DENVER, COLORADO

You are sitting in class using every last ounce of energy left from the breakfast you ate 4 hours ago, trying to keep your head from dropping onto the desktop and keeping your eyelids pried open. The teacher hurls out the words of her lecture at 100 miles per hour or more, and you begin to wonder how anyone could possibly remember all that she is telling you, let alone have time to write it all down. All you can think about is when the class will end as you stare at the clock and pray for the hands to move faster. Faster. Faster. Sound familiar? Well, if it doesn't, be prepared. High school teachers have high expectations and are not in the business to entertain you. However, while at times they may seem out to get you, teachers can sometimes become the most incredible people you will meet during your high school experience. Remember that teachers get paid less than garbage collectors and thus are not usually in the profession for the money. Instead, they honestly want to help expose you to the world and its ideas; be nice and give them a chance. Like role models, mentors, friends, and sometimes even siblings or parents, teachers can offer you necessary guidance and assistance to make your time in high school easier and more enjoyable— if you know how to deal with them and treat them. And then, of course, there remains the insignificant fact that your teachers give you grades. But no one cares about grades, right? Once you learn how to approach, understand, and react to your teachers, you'll find yourself getting along with your teachers, and the grades will surely follow.

10 TIPS FOR DEALING WITH TEACHERS

1. MAKE SURE YOUR TEACHER KNOWS YOUR NAME.

Sounds obvious, right? Yet, you would be surprised how easy it is to contract Anonymous Student Syndrome. If your teacher has to point at you and say, "Hey you, answer this question," then you're showing symptoms of the bug. During the first week of school, introduce yourself, and make certain that your teacher knows your name. You don't want the teacher filling out year-end grades without having a clue as to who you are.

I was in a block class sophomore year in which one of my teachers had a somewhat selective memory, at least for names. He was oblivious to the quiet type of student. One day, while sitting in a writing seminar session, my teacher critiqued all the papers written except for mine. He went down the list, making little marks beside the names of those who had spoken until there was only one name left, mine. He looked straight at me. Somehow my teacher couldn't believe that I was my last name. So he casually interjected into the silence, "So now, who do we have here?" I pronounced my last name, Long. "So, Long," he stated without Ms. or Miss, nothing to indicate my gender as he had done for all my classmates. Only "Long." Not only did my teacher not know my name, but he couldn't even identify what sex I was by putting my name with my face!

Then, my junior year, I think my English teacher was just scared to say my name. At the beginning of the year, she tried to pronounce it correctly, but by the end of the year she was hopelessly stuck in a rut of mispronunciation. A classmate wrote a note that she knew the teacher would read in front of the class on the pronunciation of my name. The teacher, in a little pink sweat outfit, sweetly looked at me with wide innocent eyes and said in horror, "It is said like that?"

—ANBRIT, MERCER ISLAND HIGH SCHOOL, MERCER ISLAND, WASHINGTON

2. DON'T FALL ASLEEP IN CLASS.

Easier said than done, right? Well, believe it or not, you can control your attention span within the classroom. Get a good night's sleep, if possible, and take notes in class to keep your mind processing information. Ask questions to involve yourself in the lesson and show your teacher that you are somewhat interested. Always keep your eyes open and your head off your desk. Teachers really hate it when your body language sends a message to them that you like listening to their lesson about as much as watching paint dry. As Ursula from Disney's *Little Mermaid* wisely stated, "Don't underestimate the importance of body language!"

Even if the class seems boring, try to make it exciting. Relate what your teacher is saying to your own life's experiences, or just smile and pretend that you're having fun even if you feel like pulling out your hair.

3. FIGURE OUT YOUR TEACHER'S STYLE.

All teachers portray a different image to their students. Some will try to intimidate you by not answering your questions or by covering your papers with red ink. But do not be discouraged; your teacher is just trying to get you to think for yourself. Some teachers will always lecture, while others will often separate the class into groups for small discussion or activities. Figure out the way you learn best (through visual, auditory, or some other means), so you can determine how you can (or cannot) get the information you need from your teacher. You may have to make up for differences between the way your teacher teaches and the way you learn by doing some extra reading to catch up on what you missed in class. Also, pay attention to your teacher's expectations. What kinds of questions does he ask on tests or of students in class? Does your teacher expect you to remember everything she says like a tape recorder, or just the big ideas?

4. TALK TO YOUR TEACHER IN THE HALLWAY AND AFTER CLASS.

Don't treat your teacher like some Egyptian pharaoh that sits in the front of the room on a throne of gold, cracking a whip, while you pray for the day he or she will finally be mummified and retire. Get to know your teachers. Ask conversational questions like "How are you?" (There is a fine line for this, of course—nobody likes a brown noser, including most teachers.) But more importantly, ask your teacher about the material you are studying in class. You may be amazed what insight you can get from a teacher outside of class time. After all, most teachers know what they're talking about. Furthermore, by inquiring into the class's subject material, you will show your teacher that you actually care about the class. Imagine that! It pays to speak up!

5. DON'T ASSUME A TEACHER CAN READ YOUR MIND.

Teachers do not wear radar detectors to pick up signals from stressed-out students. If you are having problems inside or outside of school and have a close relationship with a teacher, that teacher might be a good counselor. If you feel comfortable, tell your teacher about certain problems that are making it difficult for you to do your homework. Remember that teachers often have children of their own, and many are experienced in dealing with students' problems.

> *I had a teacher in tenth grade for Algebra II who wanted me to go to math competitions. But when I got into high school, I had made it a priority to diversify my activities. With cross-country and other activities, I didn't have time for math competitions. This really irked the teacher. For an entire year, we bickered back and forth, and it did neither of us any good. It turns out that I had the same teacher for my senior year. (One good thing to keep in mind: Teachers can come back to haunt you.) So I decided to just sit down with the teacher and explain that it wasn't that I didn't care about the subject, but that I just didn't have the time. I learned that teachers are people, too. You get to know a few of them and you begin to realize that they also have lives. Ever since I approached the teacher, we've had a great relationship. If you don't sit down and talk with the teacher, you're just banging your head against the wall.*
>
> —DARIN, LAKE MARY'S HIGH SCHOOL, LAKE MARY, FLORIDA

6. WHEN IN COMBAT WITH A TEACHER, FIRST CONFRONT THE ENEMY AND THEN GO FOR OUTSIDE HELP.

Don't run away from a bad relationship with a teacher. If the problem is a minor one, the best way to solve it is probably to talk to the teacher directly. Yes, this may be difficult, but if you go to someone else behind the teacher's back, he or she is likely to get angry at you (and, arguably, with good reason). If that doesn't resolve the problem, you might ask your parents or another teacher about how to proceed.

If you are having more serious problems with a teacher, such as sexual harassment, go for outside help. Some problems are best left for school counselors. Use good judgment: Don't cry wolf, but also don't let a situation get out of hand. Just because your teacher gives you a grade doesn't mean that you should put up with inappropriate behavior.

7. ALWAYS APPROACH THE TEACHER TACTFULLY WHEN YOU QUESTION HIS OR HER GRADING.

Teachers spend a lot of time grading homework, tests, quizzes, and papers. The last thing they want to discuss is mistakes in grading. Be patient! Remember how many students a teacher has: He or she is bound to make a few mistakes in grading. After all, they're all human. (Or at least some of them are!) If you think that your teacher has misjudged your work or that you deserved a different grade than what you received, approach your teacher after class one-on-one. Remember to be polite when asking your teacher to recheck your work. If your teacher rechecks your work but does not change your grade—or refuses to recheck at all—you can forget about it or seek out help. In most cases, your best plan at that point is to move on.

8. DON'T WAIT UNTIL GRADING TIME TO START SHOWING INTEREST IN THE CLASS.

A grade does not just magically appear like a genie at the end of a quarter or semester. A grade is a work in progress. If grades are important to you, don't wait until the day before your teacher turns in grades to inquire about the subject matter. Seem interested in the class from the beginning. Teachers (and students, for that matter) don't respond well to "grade grubbers," those students who always beg for higher grades. If you are active and interested in a class, chances are that your grades will be quite good at the end of the quarter or semester.

9. MAKE SURE THAT YOU GET TO KNOW AT LEAST TWO OF YOUR SOPHOMORE- OR JUNIOR-YEAR TEACHERS FOR COLLEGE RECOMMENDATIONS.

Those planning on going to college may need two teachers to write letters of recommendation. Try to figure out early on who those two teachers might be for you. Don't act differently around these two teachers, but do keep in mind that their opinion of you may have a bearing on your future.

10. BE RESPECTFUL.

Remember your audience. As friendly or informal as your relationship may be with teachers, don't forget that teachers are adults. In some Asian countries, students go so far as to bow when their instructors enter the room. You don't have to get down on the floor and scream "We're not worthy," but don't forget your manners in class. Raise your hand, don't yell out. Be helpful. Pick up your trash, and respect the teacher's rules and personal space. Ask yourself, "If I were a teacher, would I want my student to do that?" If you're uncertain about the appropriateness of a question or an action you are planning to take, always use common sense and good judgment. Treat your teachers as you hopefully would your parents or other role models.

> *Looking to the future, I know that I will never forget the influence of many of my high school teachers. The ones who taught me to write, to express my thoughts, and to think for myself will always be cherished. But above all, the ones who had confidence in me and that I could achieve have made me the person I am today. Teachers love their students more than teens realize. I hug many of my teachers on a daily basis and always greet them in the hallways, not because I want to get on their good sides, but because they have become an integral part of my life. I've found that it works best to just put yourself out there and let teachers do their magic by getting to know you as a person and as a student. It takes a special kind of person to be able to bring the best out in others. Teachers have that ability. Once they get inside of you, you won't bet able to let them out.*
>
> —SARAH, MERCER ISLAND HIGH SCHOOL, MERCER ISLAND,
> WASHINGTON

CHAPTER 9

Choosing Classes

I write for my school newspaper, and right now we're getting ready to publish an article that could easily be called, "Fletcher and the Easiest Schedule in School." This year, Fletcher, who's a senior, is challenging himself with four whole courses: ceramics, steel drum band, advanced marketing, and history. That's right, no math, no science, no English. You're probably asking, how did he do this? And more importantly, how can I get that schedule for myself?

I can't blame you for being a bit jealous of Fletcher. As I sit here, fighting through the middle of my junior year, the idea of floating through school with just a few relatively undemanding courses is more than a little appealing. However, I think that in the end it will have been worth it for me to have taken a more substantial course load. Of course, Fletcher also should be praised for picking a schedule that will make him happy, one that will allow him to enjoy his final year of high school and preserve his mental sanity as he prepares for college.

—NATHAN, MERCER ISLAND HIGH SCHOOL, MERCER ISLAND, WASHINGTON

At the other end of the spectrum from the Fletchers of high school are those people who take only honors and advanced placement (AP)

classes. They're the ones who take Analytical Calculus their freshman year, find cures for mysterious African diseases their sophomore year, and earn a Nobel Prize in literature their junior year (or the Intel/Westinghouse science prize, if they're slackers). Unfortunately, by the time many of these people have made it to their senior year, they have either of two conditions:

1. They've turned into a big ball of nerves (literally) from all the stress.

2. They've been checked into an institution for compulsive overachievers.

Most of us can agree that while taking only four classes (three of which are electives) may not be the best strategy for preparing for the future, neither is driving yourself crazy by taking a course load that would have been too hard even for Einstein (although reportedly he was never any good at school).

That's basically what this chapter is about: setting up a schedule for yourself that gets you the credits necessary to graduate, prepares you for whatever you want to do after high school, and, most importantly, fulfills you and makes high school a mostly enjoyable experience.

TIPS FOR CHOOSING CLASSES

1. GET THE CREDITS YOU NEED TO GRADUATE.

This one is fairly obvious. High school is supposed to be fun, but at the same time, it's important to make sure that you get ready for the future. To get through it, you need to pass the hurdles to graduation—namely, to obtain the credits you need before the school will let you leave with a diploma. Many schools will give you a list of exactly which courses you need to graduate; as you move through high school, you can check off what you've done and see what you still have to take. If your school doesn't hand out lists of the credits you need, find out the requirements by talking to a counselor or other informed member of the administration (see Tip 8).

Some students like to get rid of requirements (math, science, English, history, and so on) early, saving up the fun elective classes for the end of high school. By systematically completing your school's requirements, you can relax about finishing high school without having to worry about summer school or a completely full schedule the last quarter of your senior year.

> *At our high school, everyone has to take a swimming class to graduate. Alternatively, you can take a swim waiver test. My older brother had been on the swim team for years as a kid, so he thought there would be no problem with the swim test. He waited until his second semester of senior year to take it, and then he failed it because they didn't like his scissors kick! Here he was, already accepted into Harvard, and without the swim waiver he couldn't graduate from high school. He ended up having to go in and get special lessons from the PE teacher, which his friends thought was a lot funnier than he did.*
>
> —PETER, HERITAGE HIGH SCHOOL, LITTLETON, COLORADO

2. FIND COURSES THAT INTEREST YOU.

The sanity issue is clearly at work here. You've got to get the credits you need to graduate, but you need to have fun doing it. Your classes are going to take up a substantial amount of time, as will the homework assigned from them. Life is not going to be terribly enjoyable if you spend time listening to lectures and completing work about stuff that would put an insomniac to sleep. Figure out what you want to learn, and then find classes that get you credits and that interest you. You will do much better grade-wise in classes that you enjoy because studying for them will be easier.

3. FIND COURSES THAT PREPARE YOU FOR YOUR FUTURE.

Believe it or not, high school isn't an end in itself: It's a stepping stone on your way to bigger and better things. Whether your plans for after graduation include college, work, technical school, or anything else, preparation is the key. Sign up for the classes that will provide you the knowledge and the skills necessary to succeed in your future life, to the extent that you know what it is you want to do with your life. Take ceramics, if you want, but be aware that the your top-choice university probably places more importance on your understanding of physics than your ability to use a kiln (unless you're planning to study fine arts, of course). Some colleges will look at your course load in determining whether you are a good fit for that particular school.

4. SEEK VARIETY.

Variety is a good idea for a number of reasons. First, virtually every high school demands a certain depth of course variety in its graduation requirements. Second, most post-high school institutions look closely at what you've learned, and they want to see a well-rounded education. As a college admissions officer recently told an interested student, "Even if you're hoping to study only the sciences, we still need to see a foundation in English and history as well. We don't want applicants who can perform complicated experiments but can't interpret them or write coherent reports on what they've learned." Finally, taking a variety of classes ensures that you're exposed to a variety of subjects, which in turn will allow you to make a more informed decision about what you want to do after high school.

5. CHOOSE CLASSES BY TEACHER, NOT TITLE.

If you have the choice, pick the classes with the best teachers. Teachers make a course, not the other way around. After the first few weeks of school, other kids will talk about who the best teachers are. Listen. Older students are often the best sources of who to take, who is easy, who is hard, who is good, and who is drop-dead boring. The best combination is a class subject that interests you with a teacher that makes you look forward to attending class, even very early in the morning.

It was a hard decision to stick with when I chose to really challenge myself in my course choices. As time went on, I was noticeably more stressed and had less social time on my hands, and I was jealous of my friends who didn't have to deal with the same struggles I was going through. But I know that colleges aren't interested in how many nights I spent at the bowling alley, and the rest of my life will be a lot more fun if I follow the future that I want to live.

—PETER, HERITAGE HIGH SCHOOL, LITTLETON, COLORADO

6. CHALLENGE YOURSELF.

Everyone has different abilities, so what works for you may not work for your friends. But challenging yourself every so often is never a bad thing. For example, if you want to take physics but think it might be too hard, put physics together with a lighter course load and go for it.

When I received my schedule my freshman year, I was urged by more than a few upperclassmen to transfer down a level in math and science, or at least to find less demanding teachers. Their advice made me nervous, but I stuck with my schedule. I did end up receiving my lowest high school grades that first semester, but I pulled them up for the second semester and was able to finish the year with a very nice transcript. More importantly, having those hard classes taught by those hard teachers set me up very nicely for my sophomore year, and I can still feel the positive effects almost two years later. Additionally, I developed a new confidence in my ability to master new skills and challenges.

—NATHAN, MERCER ISLAND HIGH SCHOOL, MERCER ISLAND, WASHINGTON

7. Don't overload.

There is a difference between challenging yourself (see previous tip) and killing yourself. Use common sense. You know your schedule is overloaded when you have to make these concessions:

- Stay up past midnight on a regular basis to finish your homework

- Get up before 4 a.m. in the morning on a regular basis to finish your homework

- Work on homework between midnight and 4 a.m. in the morning on a regular basis

If you have to sacrifice sleep or happiness to keep up with class work, you've probably gone overboard. Don't let yourself get burned out or sick because you are taking a schedule that is too difficult. Challenge yourself within reason.

8. Make a master plan.

With your school's list of requirements in hand, chart your course through high school. Write down, semester by semester, the classes you *want* to take and the classes you *need* to take. Your list shouldn't be set in stone, but it's a good idea to have one as a guide for your four years. When you're figuring out what your schedule should be like for a certain term, it's really convenient to have a map telling you exactly where you should be and in what direction you are going.

9. Talk to your counselor.

Counselors get paid to help you with your course schedule and questions such as the ones we're raising here: Use them to your advantage. Ask them which classes are best for college preparation and life after high school. Does the college you might be interested in require a foreign language? How much college credit do you get for AP classes? These are the types of questions counselors should be able to answer. Some counselors are better than others; as with teachers, seek out the best counselors. If you are assigned to a counselor that is not as good, try to ask specific questions that you know he or she can be helpful in answering.

By the way, some colleges and other post-high school institutions are interested in what your counselor has to say about you, and it's better if he or she can write "John Doe is a conscientious student who has impressed me with his ambition," rather than "John Doe? That's the kid who signed up for three periods of PE last semester, right?"

10. TALK TO OLDER STUDENTS AND LISTEN TO THEIR ADVICE.

> *Perhaps one of the smartest things I've done in the past year is recruit Annie as my personal mentor. Annie is a year older than me. She's a great student, a great tennis player, and a good all-around role model. I hate to use the phrase "role model" because for so many people it conjures up the image of some dorky, annoyingly wholesome Boy Scout, but that's what she is. No, not a Boy Scout. What I mean is that she's someone I really respect and to whom I enjoy listening about the struggles she faces and the struggles I will face a year from now. It was Annie who guided me through the torture that was chemistry, and it is she who now gives me daily advice about applying for college. Annie is someone I hope to emulate, academically, athletically, and otherwise.*
>
> —NATHAN, MERCER ISLAND HIGH SCHOOL, MERCER ISLAND, WASHINGTON

Older students are often your best source for good information about teachers, colleges, social gatherings, and so on. Counselors may not have the straight scoop, but older students know the gossip. They know the hard graders and the easier ones. They know which coach gives new kids a shot and which ones only play their starting team. If you know an older student, ask for advice. We promise it will be useful.

11. MAKE YOURS A UNIQUE COURSE LOAD.

You're unique, just like everyone else. Find your own niche. Some students love English and history, so they rightfully choose to fill their schedules with those courses—besides the requisite math and science classes, of course. You might enjoy foreign languages, so take a couple of those as well. You may or may not have the same interests or abilities as the kids who get really into chemistry or math; your schedule should reflect that.

SOME FINAL THOUGHTS . . .

So, there you have it. That's all our worldly advice about classes, counselors, challenges, and everything else that has to do with high school schedules. Work hard, but not too hard. Take interesting classes, but take some math, too. Choosing the right classes is essential to having fun and learning a lot during the next four years of your life. These classes will teach you much of the important, interesting information you'll need in high school and beyond. Choose wisely.

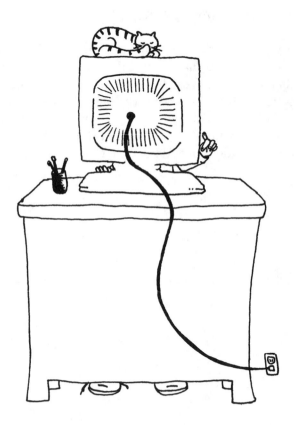

CHAPTER 10

Computers and the Internet

Admit it, you need a "fix." The temptation is just too hard to resist. Leave your parents, siblings, and classmates behind and enter a private, plugged-in world of potential addiction. No, we're not talking illicit drug use here. We're referring to the magnetic pull of your keyboard and the darkened computer screen that draws you ever closer. It's ready to tap into your time, social life, and brain cells.

Forget the Pepsi Generation; we are undeniably the Computer Generation. Many of us began our computer bonding in a little chair at a small kindergarten table. Cute little kids and computer technology have grown up together, and young people undoubtedly rule the computer scene. Ironically, many of us are more computer-literate than our teachers or parents. Computers are our private link to our friends and the outside world. Increasingly, they serve as our major tool for high school homework. Onscreen word processing, editing, electronic spell-checking, and built-in thesauruses have made us dependent upon computers. What high school or city libraries once provided our parents in the way of research, our Mac, IBM-compatible, or laptop now lets us do from the comfort of our family room or bedroom.

We know the familiar program lingo: Microsoft Word, Word Perfect, Excel, ClarisWorks, America Online, and Yahoo! We can compose—or can readily learn how to create—spreadsheets, graphics, desktop publishing, charts, CD, and online/Internet research. But there's one bottom line: We will be eternally grateful to the computer gods who developed word-processing software. We'll use it for every term paper we have to do for the rest of our lives.

Check Out Your Resources . . .

During the first days of high school, you should find a couple minutes of time to visit your school's computer lab, if your school has one. Whether it has Pentium or Power Macintosh computers, color inkjet or laser printers, get to know the systems and find out what software and programs the lab has. The vast majority of schools will have computers in place with Internet access.

What Computers Can Do

In the *Star Trek* TV show, Captain Kirk challenged mankind "to boldly go where no man has gone before." Computers offer the same open-ended prospect for papers, research, entertainment, communication, and electronic relationships. With time, practice, and software tutorials, you can impress your teachers with some sophisticated computer fancywork that will most likely improve your efficiency in school—and might eventually improve your GPA.

SOFTWARE, SOFTWARE, SOFTWARE

Most newer computers now automatically come with good combination software programs that enable word processing and communication software. Most newer computers also are multimedia-capable. Not only can you write an English essay, but you can also listen to Dave Matthews on the CD drive simultaneously. Thousands of programs come on CD-ROM rather than a pile of floppy discs. Entire encyclopedias, thousands of clip art images, and the oldie-but-goody *National Geographic* magazine have put their entire contents on CD-ROMs.

PRINTERS

But wait, we can't forget that unassuming machine sitting beside your hard drive or monitor. A good printer can turn an average paper into an average paper that looks good. Don't use the Draft setting when you are printing a final draft of a paper to turn in for a grade: Presentation counts for something.

COMPUTERS IN OUR LIVES

Perhaps you have heard your parents tell how in the olden days they had to research their homework in the school library (way before copy machines) and hand-write reams of penciled notes in spiral-bound notebooks. You can bet they spent many homework nights copying information out of the *Encyclopedia Britannica,* now stored in the basement of your grandparents' home. If the plug was pulled on the nation's computers, every high school student in the United States would be on their knees: We can't live without them. We have bonded with cyberspace, and there's no turning back. Here are a few tips for better coping with the ever-changing computer age.

LEARN TO TYPE

If you aren't a good keyboarder yet, make it a priority—you will have a tough time with the hunt-and-peck method in high school, let alone college and the great beyond. Through your school or a software program, you definitely need to learn how to type relatively quickly and error-free. Typed papers are easier to read and more professional looking than hand-written materials. What's more, there's a good chance that a neatly typed homework assignment will mean a higher grade for you.

BEWARE YOUR SPELL-CHECKER

Thank your lucky stars that some computer programmer created spell-checking software. A word of warning: These programs will identify commonly misspelled words but not misused words, which means they can't distinguish between *there* and *their, which* and *witch, night* and *knight, now* and *know,* and so on. Don't rely on spell-check alone. Proofread every piece of word-processed homework you type for incorrect words. You also can find some grammar-check programs, but keep in mind that the computer doesn't know what you're trying to say, so don't necessarily go along with all of its suggestions. As a rule, you should always double-check for punctuation, grammar, and spelling before you hand anything to a teacher.

COMPUTE AND SURF AT SCHOOL

If you've got some time to kill in study hall, or if you have an unexpected free period, don't always blow those minutes hanging out with your friends or getting off campus. Head to the computer lab and get some homework done. Even if you have a computer at home, don't always count on computer time at home each night. You may have to share your computer with your little brother who has a big third-grade bug report due the next day. Or, if your dad has business reports to type up or e-mail to check that night, your homework might not be the highest priority.

IF YOU'RE DOING HOMEWORK ON THE COMPUTER, FOCUS ON THE WORK

Don't do computer homework while doing something else. You know, avoid the usual problem areas: talking on the phone, listening to the radio, or watching *Monday Night Football* on TV. This is not the time to be instant-messaging your friends on AOL. Make your computer homework a focused priority, and schedule the three-way phone chats and tube time for later. Also avoid bringing a lot of food and drink around the computer. If the keys crunch every time you type, you may regret eating that package of cookies the night before.

SAVE YOUR WORK OFTEN

Back up your work every 10 minutes! Many a horror story has happened when some unfortunate victim neglected to save his text. The family cat might unexpectedly jump onto your keyboard to get in your lap and in the process step on the wrong command key. Or, your younger brother might want to get in a quick game of Civilization II while your mom isn't watching. If you haven't saved your Pulitzer Prize–winning essay to your disk or hard drive, it's history. Repeat after me, "I will back up my work every 10 minutes!"

> *I had just finished my Spanish paper (and not saved it yet), when I realized that I forgot to add some of the accents. I asked a friend to show me the commands. She came in and proceeded to press a series of keys, which instantly cleared everything on my screen. I was frantic and tried desperately to undo what she had just done, but it was too late. I was stuck retyping my entire paper.*
>
> —TANYA, PHILLIPS ACADEMY, ANDOVER, MASSACHUSETTS

BEFRIEND A COMPUTER JOCK

These people's interests may not include athletics, music, student government, or the debate club. They can be shy and reclusive in the school cafeteria, and you may never see them on the weekends, but these classmates—and potential friends—are computer wizards ready and willing to give you cyberhelp. Seek one of them out and start a conversation—one day he or she may electronically save your life. While you were watching *Gilligan's Island* reruns on Nickelodeon or doing the couch potato routine with MTV, the computer jocks were learning how to format discs, write their own software, and install their own computer chip memory boards. With the promise of a pizza or just a friendly chat, these computer experts can make house calls to install your new software programs. Or, they can bail you out late at night when you think your essay has been zapped from your laptop's memory. Ever wonder what Bill Gates' classmates thought of him back in high school?

GIVE YOURSELF AND YOUR COMPUTER SOME BREAKS

If you're starting to suffer from gridlock or your eyes are glazing over from staring at the monitor for hours, it's time to take a break. Make sure you have enough light to do your work, and grab a good chair if you are in for a long night at the computer.

Don't forget to turn off your computer when you are done. Keeping your computer on at all times increases the likelihood of future trouble. Give your computer a chance to rest when you are not on duty.

TREAT YOUR COMPUTER WITH RESPECT

Keep your computer and printer in a cool place, not perched on top of a radiator. Put your drinks and snacks far away from it to avoid accidental spills and greasy keyboards. You haven't lived until you've used a box of Q-tips trying to get Dr. Pepper out of your keyboard or until you've tried to quickly mop up spills from under your hard drive. Try to keep your computer area neat. The same rules apply for laptops.

By the way, don't hit your computer—physical abuse tends to backfire. If you have just lost your entire paper and feel like hitting something, find a punching bag or take a jog. Next time you will remember to save your work more often.

I was up late one night trying to finish typing a history paper, which was due the next day. I was drinking soda and eating tons of candy to try and stay awake to finish it. I was not thinking and decided to place my soda can right next to my laptop as I reached across my desk for another candy bar. As luck would have it, my sleeve got caught on the pop can, and it poured out all over my laptop keyboard. I flipped out and grabbed a box of Kleenex frantically trying to avoid an electronic disaster. That night I was lucky and my computer turned out fine, but from then on I make a point of keeping all food and drink off my desk!

—LAUREN, PHILLIPS ACADEMY, ANDOVER, MASSACHUSETTS

USE SURGE PROTECTION

An electronic surge in your home or at school may be more than a temporary inconvenience: If your computer is on, it can mean disaster. Your word-processed English paper could be permanently lost in cyberspace as a result. If your parents have not already bought a surge protector, splurge. Save up a few dollars and head to the nearest electronics store to find out what you need.

TEST OUT THE GAMES AND E-MAIL

Sure, we're all sleep-deprived teenagers because of school, home, or even job responsibilities. But once the pressure of homework is done, it's time to let loose. Computer games are great—so is e-mail. Try out the latest programs. Send your friends e-mail messages, but remember how easy it is to forward messages to other people. Don't write anything in an e-mail that you wouldn't want repeated to your boyfriend, enemy, parents, or teachers. The phone doesn't leave as much of a trace.

GET A LIFE

Don't let the computer take over your life. The computer can be like an electronic black hole sucking up your time, energy, and high school social life. No question about it, computers are amazing learning tools and entertainment outlets. Just keep a balance between your time on the computer and real-life face-to-face learning. Once in a while, opt for the hand-written letter instead of the quick e-mail. Be interactive with your classmates, too. Your friends, not the computer, will be the true key to helping you successfully survive high school.

THE INTERNET AND THE WORLD WIDE WEB

The information superhighway is out there, and we've started our engines. We have a license to surf the net 24 hours a day. Nearly every person, place, or thing in the world can be researched, downloaded, linked, or printed from the Internet with the push of a button. In school assignments, most teachers will stick to scholarly subjects for you to investigate via the Internet. Computer search engines such as Yahoo!, Lycos, Excite, Alta Vista, Hotbot, or Dogpile can bring up information on almost any obscure subject your teacher can throw at you.

Need a current article on Mexican politics for history tomorrow? Get online and find today's issue of the country's largest newspaper in Spanish or English.

Want to know the status of the Mars Pathfinder vehicle in a galaxy far away? Check out NASA's home page for the details, and download recent photos of the Martian landscape.

Need to summarize the major works of Ernest Hemingway or John Steinbeck? Point your mouse to the *Reader's Guide to Periodic Literature.*

Don't forget to access large city or college libraries that are brimming with statistics, book reviews, sound bytes, and music.

Once your homework is done, the fun really begins. Turn on your computer and start surfing. Any time, day or night, an endless Internet world stands ready to inform and entertain you. For you conspiracy theorists, check out one of the thousands of *X-Files* sites that rehash every episode.

Want to add some free art to your bedroom wall? Download and print a photo of Cindy Crawford, Michael Jordan, or Monet's water lilies. Who knows where one Web site will take you when you click on related or linked subjects.

Computer lovers also can design a personal home page. The Internet can flash your innermost thoughts around the world in seconds, and you could even become famous.

Be careful, though. The Internet is home to many a weirdo and scam artist. Don't agree to meet strange people at strange places, and don't give out personal information. Keep it fun, but keep it safe.

> *One time, my friend and I decided to arrange to meet with this guy we had been communicating with over the Net. He seemed totally harmless, and since we lived fairly close, we decided to meet and catch a movie. Well, we did, and it wasn't like he was some guy who escaped from the federal penitentiary or anything. Still, he was just kind of slimy, and he kept trying to kiss and grab my friend, even after she'd been pushing him away. We ended up walking out of the movie because he was such a loser. We even felt somewhat threatened by the way he was coming on so strong. Now we're trying to stop communicating with him. I really wish we hadn't gotten together with him at all— it's so much better to know the guy before you give him your address.*
>
> —Eloise, SCECGS, Sydney, Australia

A final note about the Internet and the World Wide Web: It's never too early for you to begin the college research process. The Internet has made this easier than ever. You can still request the glossy, colorful brochures to be sent by mail, but it is much easier to find a school's home page and read the promotional facts and figures there. Application requests for information via the Internet are often processed faster than those arriving by mail. In some cases, you can even take virtual tours of the campus. The sites often are so helpful that you can get a head start on your high school guidance counselor and research the college scene before your senior year. (For more information, check out Chapter 25, "College Application Process.")

COMPUTER AND INTERNET USE (AND ABUSE)

This will never make David Letterman's show, but here's a Top-10 List of Computer Don'ts.

10. Don't steal computer software (it's against the law).

9. Don't hack into your school's files (duh!).

8. Don't use offensive language online to degrade others—including teachers—unless you are dying to get caught.

7. Don't charge fees to your school or someone else's online account.

6. Don't give out personal information about yourself or a friend to bulletin boards, chat rooms, or anywhere else on the Internet.

5. Don't sabotage files or disks that are not your own.

4. Don't load, download, store, send, or print material that harasses or discriminates against anyone in school.

3. Don't use the computer system, Internet, or school phone system for commercial or illegal purposes.

2. Don't download, distribute, or keep computer-generated pornography or other questionable material at school.

1. Don't plagiarize from online materials: It's the same as plagiarizing from printed materials.

School computer usage is a privilege, not a right, so try to follow these rules. Plagiarism is probably the rule most often broken, but teachers and administrators take it very seriously. If you pull information from the Internet and copy it word-for-word, or even copy major ideas from a written or Internet source, you must cite it accordingly and attribute the words and ideas to an author and source. (When in doubt, include the Web address where you found the material.) Anyway, it looks better when you cite sources—you sound more intelligent, and it proves you did some research.

GO CRAZY

Computers are changing and getting better all the time. Spend some time learning about this most important tool. Surf the Web. Try out new games. Maybe even design a home page for yourself and your family. If you start viewing the computer as a friend, the time you spend writing long essays won't be as lonely.

CHAPTER 11

Athletics

> *Sports are a very healthy way to spend your high school years because this gives you an opportunity to release some of the stress of school. In addition, you can interact with and meet kids in your grade and other grade levels who have the same interest as you do. I play tennis and have come to know people around the state who I would never have known otherwise. Although I am from Morgan City, Louisiana, whenever I go to New Orleans, I meet people who I have seen or played with in tennis tournaments. It's a great feeling to have this immediate bond. Without knowing anything about each other, we can immediately become friends because we share the interest in tennis.*
>
> —JONATHAN, MORGAN CITY, LOUISIANA

While many people are aware of the far-reaching benefits of high school athletics, they may be quick to give up these rewards because they fear that terrible word: commitment. Although the idea of commitment in sports is not a misconception, there are a number of ways to accept the commitment and to enjoy yourself through the many long, hard hours of practice and sacrifice.

SELECTING THE SPORT

Whatever you do, choose a sport that you enjoy, one that you are willing to work hard at to improve and excel. Don't select your sport by choosing what your friends like. Don't choose something you are good at but don't enjoy. Don't choose a sport because the coach is your physics teacher and you think he will pass you if you play for him.

Choose a sport that excites you. This advice applies equally to school and to intramural sports. If you hate the idea of being outside and getting your hair messed up, then soccer isn't the sport for you. If you have a bladder problem, then swimming is probably your safest sport (no one will ever know) but maybe not your favorite. High school sports take a lot of time and energy, and you don't want to dedicate yourself to something that doesn't float your boat. Also, know your schedule and the schedule of the sport you plan to join so that you can make sure your other activities don't conflict with practice, games, or meets.

> *"Run for fun?" my friends always ask, mockingly. No one can quite understand why I put myself through hours of pain each day and then give up my weekends to prepare for and participate in meets. But running is my passion. I love to run. I love the team and I love to put myself through those hours of pain. I can't say that I love to give up my Saturday mornings (I'm not that weird), but it's worth it to me, no matter how much ridicule I receive.*
>
> —LAUREN, ISADORE NEWMAN HIGH SCHOOL,
> NEW ORLEANS, LOUISIANA

GETTING ALONG WITH THE COACH

An important element of high school athletics (not intramurals) is interaction with the coach. It's up to you, the athlete, whether to make the coach a friend or an enemy. Make sure to earn the coach's respect and to show the coach that you respect him or her. If you have any problems or complaints about the way he or she runs your team, be sure to tell the coach diplomatically and in private. It will bring down the whole spirit of the team if this is done in the open, and the whole team may latch on to your negative attitude, which will only make things worse. Treat the coach as you would treat a boss: Make your opinions known, but do it respectfully.

> *When I tried out for the varsity soccer team at my school, I knew I was prepared physically and mentally for the team. I had worked hard all summer long and had given everything in me to becoming an outstanding soccer player. When the coach held tryouts, he neglected to even look in my direction. I knew I was playing well, but he didn't care. The coach called all my friends and told them that they made the team. He didn't even call me to tell me I was cut. I was so upset about the whole thing that I wanted to run up and punch the coach in the face. My parents told me that wasn't such a good idea. Instead, I wrote the coach a letter thanking him for letting me try out and I told him that I would be his team's "number one fan." The next year, I was the first player who was called and invited on the team.*
>
> —SARAH, NEW YORK, NEW YORK

IMPORTANCE OF NUTRITION AND REST

When you become a team member, it is important to commit yourself fully to the team. Commitment not only means going to practices and games, but also eating and sleeping well during the season. When you want to reach over and finish off a plate of delicious homemade cookies, just think of how great an apple tastes. When all your friends are out partying late, think of how lucky you are to be able to go home and get into your warm, soft bed. Although you may be annoyed by this at times, it definitely pays off in the long run. We know (or at least hope) that all high school students are too young to drink legally, but sometimes high-schoolers are confronted with cigarettes, alcohol, and drugs. These seemingly harmless substances can hinder your performance; be sure to keep your goals in sight at all times.

Additionally, steroids may seem like the perfect solution to your inability to lift as much as that starter on your team. But it is so important to know the long-term effects of such a powerful drug. In addition to the immediate rages, temper problems, and effects on personality, steroids can seriously hinder your heart, kidneys, and other important body parts. Don't be stupid.

COPING WITH INJURIES

Injuries are no fun. Not only are they painful, but they can also set you back from your training. But realize that injuries are not the end of the world. Focus on the positive—your injury will give you some time to rest and relax before going at it 100 percent when the injury heals. It is essential to treat your injury as soon as it surfaces. Visit the athletic trainer or a doctor, and find out exactly what to do to make it better. Some people may get the urge to call you a wimp for not playing with a minor injury, but you are better off taking a couple of days to recover earlier in the season than to be out for weeks at a time.

Be sure not to let your inability to participate dampen your spirits. Make a point to go and cheer at every game you can't play in and to show up for every team dinner or activity. Show your mental commitment when your physical commitment is on standby.

BALANCING SCHOOL, EXTRACURRICULARS, AND SPORTS

High school is a tough time in everyone's life. It often seems that no matter how well you balance your time, you never have a free moment. With school, the band, student council, and the service club, who has time to play basketball as well? But it is important to realize that everyone is busy. The key to a more enjoyable high school experience is learning how to balance your time. Most people find that the more activities they have to do, the more productive and organized they become. Be sure to remember your priorities and not to let one activity overshadow another. Don't take on too much at one time.

HOW TO COPE WITH NOT STARTING

No one likes to spend hours each day practicing and then warming the bench for the entire game. Still, this is something that most everyone must experience at one time or another. Not many people start out at the top, so you have to expect to start somewhere. Don't give up when you are not playing, though. Your position on the bench is an important stage in your high school sports career. This is where you have to show your coach how committed you are to your team and how much you care about the sport. No coach likes a whiny pouter. If you show the coach your determination and maturity, you will force him or her to think about giving you more playing time.

> *I worked so hard on my baseball skills. When I was in middle school, my dad and I would wake up every morning and shovel snow away from the driveway so I could hit the ball before school. No one worked as hard as I did, so when my coach benched me the first three games of my season, I was devastated. At first I just gave up, claiming that my hard work had done nothing. But then I realized the importance of never quitting. I showed the coach my enthusiasm and determination and asked him for suggestions on improving my swing. Soon I was playing in all the games; by the end of the season, I was starting.*
>
> —PHIL, MINNEAPOLIS, MINNESOTA

HANDLING WINNING AND LOSING

Not many people like losing—you might have heard the old expression, "Show me a good loser and I'll show you a loser." But, in every competition, there is bound to be a loser—and maybe even more than one. Losing requires a great deal of responsibility. This is the point when you have to hold your head high (but not too high), shake hands with opponents, and show your team's mental strength. After a loss, it is easy to feel like giving up, but the best athletes and teams see it otherwise. Losing a game can be taken as a step backward, or it can be taken as an opportunity to learn from mistakes and improve. When you find yourself on a losing team, remember that your approach to the loss affects how other people see it: The more positive your attitude, the more likely you are to increase your team's capacity to move on in a positive way.

Being a good winner is also as important as being a good loser. If you gloat in your opponent's face, then your opponent will see you not as a superior athlete, but as an arrogant juvenile. The most intimidating winners are the ones who take it in stride: Act like you have been there before.

RESPONSIBILITIES OF THE CAPTAIN

There is no higher honor than to be selected by your peers or your coach to serve as captain of your team. For the most part, this honor goes to seniors and is a reward for years of previous service and commitment. Along with this honor comes the responsibility of leadership. Yes, it's the captain who goes out to participate in the coin toss and to accept the trophy for winning the game, tournament, or championship, but it is also the captain who has the responsibility of leading the team when morale is down after losing several games, matches, or races. The captain has the responsibility for the phone tree when a practice or meet is canceled or the coach wants to send an immediate message to the team. Captains are also helpful in assisting younger players to transition from neophytes to top competitors.

Finally, captains are the glue that hold the team together. Invariably, the team will face problems and obstacles during the season. Captains are expected to have the maturity to keep the team on an even keel, not getting too excited about a victory or too upset following a loss or defeat.

Scholarship Opportunities

Outstanding high school athletes will often have an opportunity to continue their athletic careers in college. Some high school standouts will even be offered a scholarship for their athletic skills. If a scholarship is of interest to you, make sure that your coach is aware of your plans because he or she can be an invaluable asset in connecting you with college coaches and recruiters. Be sure to save all your newspaper clippings that record your accolades and any videotapes that demonstrate your fine form. If a recruiter is watching you play, make an effort to meet him or her after the contest. Be gracious. Send thank-you letters and acknowledge all correspondence to colleges or universities that contact you about a scholarship.

Enjoying Your Sport

Never forget that the most important aspect of high school sports is having fun. Participating in sports is the part of the day that you should be excited and enthused about, not the part that you are dreading or hoping to avoid. You can't be committed to a sport that you don't enjoy, and you can't succeed in a sport without commitment.

Participating in sports can be one of the highlights of your high school life. For those of you who may go on to participate at a higher level in sports, you have to start somewhere. Hopefully, these tips will take you to the top. For the rest of us mortals, high school athletics is a special and rare opportunity to compete hard and have fun. Take advantage of every minute of it, and enjoy the camaraderie and as well as the competition.

CHAPTER 12

Extracurriculars: A Salvation from the Grind

While constructing the class float for the homecoming parade, the clear sky was suddenly taken over by ominous clouds that looked ready to burst. Unable to continue working on the float, people started playing catch and other field games within our limits of the driveway. Since we were all having so much fun, we decided to meet back at Kara's house, near the high school, that night, clad in scrubby clothes for a gruesome game of Smear the Queer in The Jungle (the high school football field). So, promptly at 8:00, everyone arrived looking like unbathed, ungroomed, giddy fourth-graders. We tromped through the puddles to The Jungle and, as soon as we made it to the field, everyone went crazy. People were running, rolling, somersaulting, and sliding everywhere. I have never had so much fun playing in the mud! Unfortunately, our games were cut short when a bored policeman suspected that we goofy teenagers were up to no good. He shined his flashlight on us and looked at us mud-covered kids with disbelief. Surprisingly, he didn't

> *chide us but merely laughed and told us to go home. With spirits still high, we all returned to Kara's to change, drink hot chocolate, and watch movies into the wee hours of the night. I can't wait for the float committee next year!*
>
> —Jennifer, Mercer Island High School, Mercer Island, Washington

Why Should You Get Involved?

Where would you be without extracurricular activities? These activities give you an escape from school, a chance to discover your interests, and an opportunity to meet friends. After all, a high school student shouldn't spend every waking moment after school studying. How boring! That would be like taking all the sugar out of candy. Not only are extracurriculars a salvation, but they are an essential ingredient in the recipe for having a fun, successful high school career.

So, Why Are Extracurriculars So Great?

1. Friends

Generally, the people who are your best friends are people with whom you share similar interests. Getting involved in activities gives you a chance to meet interesting people: Who knows, that shy girl on your soccer team may end up becoming a close friend.

Also consider participating in activities outside of school. You might meet some new friends from your own school as well as people from other schools you never would have met otherwise.

> *By singing in a choir outside of school, I have met many girls who have become my good friends. On the surface none of us are the same, and if I saw them*

> *walking down the hall at school I probably wouldn't give them a second thought. Only meeting outside of school because of a shared interest made me stop and get to know them.*
>
> —KARA, MERCER ISLAND HIGH SCHOOL,
> MERCER ISLAND, WASHINGTON

2. FUN

Honestly, how many people never get bored of reading and studying? Countless memories are created from activities and experiences. You're more likely to remember that amazing touchdown at the homecoming game than the answer to number three on the math final.

3. STRESS RELIEF

Everyone has had days when they come home from school wanting to tear out their hair. Sometimes the high school grind gets so monotonous that it's hard to stay focused. Although extracurriculars aren't always the solution, they sure can help because they give you a chance to loosen up, relax, and take your mind off the major lab due tomorrow. Taking a study break to help paint the sets for the school play can make you return to studying on a high note. True, having more activities to be involved in fills up your schedule, but it often makes you more organized and a better manager of time. A lot of students who participate in extracurriculars will tell you, "The more things I have to do, the better I plan my day."

> *Out of school, I participate in any form of drama I can get my hands on. It's important to make friends outside of school, but for me that's not the most important part. I need to escape from school, push away the work for a little while, and have a chance to sit back and breathe.*
>
> —BRIAN, BENTLEY SCHOOL, BERKELEY, CALIFORNIA

4. LEARNING

Yes, it may sound corny, but learning is definitely an aspect of extracurricular activities. Becoming involved helps you discover what your personal strengths and weaknesses are and helps you find your niche. Keep in mind that not everything can be learned from a book: You can't read the driving guide and hop into the driver's seat for the first time expecting to drive flawlessly. Experiences that you have in extracurricular activities will enable you to learn a lot about yourself.

5. YOUR RESUME

Extracurriculars can help guide you toward future career paths or colleges because they let you discover if you're truly interested in a certain field. Extracurriculars also build character traits, including leadership and cooperation, which are very important in the hunt for a career—and in life in general.

Extracurriculars can open doors of opportunity; many students earn college scholarships because of an area in which they excel, such as sports, writing, or business. Lastly, extracurriculars can add depth to you college application or job resume. Colleges and employers look for experience and uniqueness; someone with a 4.0 and the personality of a box of rocks may not get as far.

6. GOALS

Goals are important to have all the time because they give you a sense of direction. Personal aspirations are more motivating than having someone shout commands at you. Goals and incentives can help you stay dedicated and keep you on task, even when you feel like your eyelids are made of lead. As in school, you have to be committed and try hard to succeed in extracurriculars. Unless you're Michael Jordan's little brother, you probably won't make the state-winning varsity basketball team without ever practicing or focusing. You can make goals long-term ("I will run for class president at the end of the year") or short-term ("I will finish all my homework before band practice") to give you motivation. It's always rewarding to attain a goal.

What Can You Get Involved In?

Most high schools offer a wide variety of activities or clubs to join. If your school doesn't offer something of interest to you, some other organization probably sponsors the activity that caters to your needs. High school is the perfect time for you to experiment and try all sorts of different things. If modern dance sounds fun to you, go for it! Who cares if you've never learned a step of dance before?

If You Are Having Trouble Finding the Right Activity for You, You May Want to Try:

1. Sports

If you've heard the phrase "strong mind, strong body," you probably know that sports keep you active—even if they don't give you those to-die-for rippling muscles. You can also make new friends or become closer with old friends. You don't have to make varsity to have fun and play well, either: If you've never played a certain sport before but want to try, do it.

Involvement in school sports gives you a sense of school spirit, pride, and belonging as well. It's fun to dress up in school colors—and, besides, you feel awesome wearing that sweat-stained, dirty football jersey to school on days of home games.

2. Service clubs

If you're a do-gooder interested in charity work, your school probably has some program for you. The counselors at your school might have information about a certain charity needing help on a certain occasion, but if you're looking for volunteering on a more regular basis, service clubs are the answer. Service clubs often help out at local charities and put on food, toy, or health-supply drives. Service clubs are a good way to give back to your community, and charity work is much more rewarding than sitting around watching re-runs on TV.

> *My first job for the Driscoll Diplomats, a service club,*
> *required me to get up real early on a Sunday morning*
> *to go to school just to serve people pancakes for a*
> *breakfast fundraiser. I didn't really look forward to*
> *getting up at the crack of dawn on a weekend, but since*
> *I joined the group to get out of school a few days of the*
> *year for field trips, I figured it was worth it. As it*
> *turned out though, joining the group made me new*
> *friends, and helping out at the breakfast wasn't so bad*
> *after all. Now, normally you think of people who go to*
> *"all you can eat" buffets to be these big, beefy dudes,*
> *but a little guy was the one who seemed to be enjoying*
> *himself the most. Each time I passed him, which*
> *must've been 15 times, the little guy asked for "about*
> *four more." I tried to guess how many pancakes he'd*
> *eaten, but I think after 50 it really doesn't matter. I*
> *guess you could consider that a little on the disgusting*
> *side, but the guy looked to me like he was having a*
> *pretty good time. I'm looking forward to the more*
> *memorable experiences ahead that I'll have as a*
> *Diplomat I'm sure, but I'll always remember that*
> *"pancake man."*
>
> —Matt, Driscoll High School, Glendale Heights, Illinois

3. Interest Clubs

One bulletin in the high school morning announcement reads: "Do you like science but are afraid your friends might find out? Come to the science club meeting in room 109 after school. Free food." Although your picture of this group might include stereotypical scrawny science-loving boys with suspenders and thick glasses, the science club may actually be full of hard-working, interested members—including brawny athletes—who get together regularly to work on projects for regional competitions. Art club, math club, international club, business club, and the committee to save the earth are some popular clubs found at many high schools. These clubs are a good place to meet people with interests similar to your own. After all, it's unlikely that someone who hates math will be attending a math club meeting. Among the benefits of joining clubs, you get to have fun doing something you enjoy, you get to meet people with common interests, you don't face too big of a commitment, and, of course, you might get free food.

4. Music

For the musically inclined, band and orchestra are great activities to consider. Offered as a class in most schools, this activity takes a commitment outside of school as well. Marching practice for half-time shows and practicing solos or tricky pieces can be time-consuming, but the outcome is worthwhile. Band is a chance to show school pride—and those starchy uniforms really aren't all that uncomfortable.

5. Drama

Many celebrities started off their acting careers with roles in high school plays, so you never know where this could lead. Drama takes guts, so it's not for the timid or for introverts. Not only do you have to dedicate a lot of your time, but you also have to stand up in front of the entire student body and perform. Most schools offer a drama class that requires time after school as well. If your school doesn't offer drama courses, check with your counselor (or with the Yellow Pages) to see if there is a local youth theater where you might be able to audition.

6. Student government

Another great way to show school pride is to be an active member of student government. Helping organize dances and assemblies is almost as fun as actually going. This helps build leadership and cooperation skills, which are used continually. Like most activities, however, student government is time-consuming because it involves campaigning, orating, attending meetings and conferences, and working with peers.

> *I didn't realize how much time commitment was involved in Associate Student Body when I ran for class secretary. Because my class was put in charge of putting on the homecoming dance, we had meetings*

> *every day after school, which meant that I would be late to crew or ended up studying really late. None of the officers really understood what we had to do, so it was kind of hectic. But after much stress and chaos, the final result was something to be quite proud of.*
>
> —JENNIFER, MERCER ISLAND HIGH SCHOOL, MERCER ISLAND, WASHINGTON

7. START YOUR OWN CLUB

If none of the clubs offered at your school appeal to you but you have something incredible in mind, form your own club. To organize your own club, you must first have an idea. You can talk to your class advisor, who will probably ask you why you want to start this club, so have some reasons ready. If you're given the okay to do so, decorate the school halls with appealing posters and spread news by word of mouth. You will need to organize a place to have meetings and make sure that people know when and where to go, so have all that worked out before you tell everyone about the club.

> *At my school, people can start clubs easily. The sophomore class officers organized S.C.I.A., Sophomore Class In Action, to help organize and put on fund-raisers. A group of seniors formed the Seinfeld Club, which is a chance to watch different episodes during lunch. Even a couple students put on their own field trip to go roller skating! Forming your own club just takes an idea and some patience.*
>
> —JENNIFER, MERCER ISLAND HIGH SCHOOL, MERCER ISLAND, WASHINGTON

Getting Involved

HOW DO YOU GET INVOLVED?

If you know what you want to get involved in, find out information about when and where the first meeting will be held. This information can be obtained from posters, teachers, morning announcements, or word of mouth. If you want to find out about the swim team, you can ask the team captain or some member any questions you have. For school sports, you will have to fill out release and health forms, so be sure to sign up by the deadline. For most interest and service clubs, getting involved just means going to the meetings. If you are interested in getting involved in drama or music, you must sign up for the class or talk to the teacher. Getting involved doesn't take much time, but make sure you know your calendar.

HOW MUCH TIME DO EXTRACURRICULARS TAKE?

Depending on what you choose to pursue, time commitment varies. The workload from classes in high school is usually a lot heavier than in middle school or junior high, and the expectations from teachers are also a lot higher. However, this doesn't mean that from the moment school is out until the moment you fall asleep you will have to be doing homework. It just means that you have to organize your time carefully and know your priorities.

Sports teams usually practice every day after school for a couple of hours. It's a pretty big commitment because missing a practice can mean not playing in the big game on Friday. Service and interest clubs don't demand a lot of your time, but they will occasionally have a big event, such as a day spent collecting and sorting donations from a food drive or a big competition. Drama and music can require a fair amount of time as well. During football season, band is a big commitment, but you also get into football games free. Rehearsals can seem endless, but they're usually worth all the time and effort. Student government can be really busy, too, before dances and school activities. As long as you understand how to organize your time, however, it is possible to pull off a busy schedule of sports, clubs, and school.

WILL EXTRACURRICULARS HARM YOUR GRADES?

Rather than harming a student's school progress, it has been shown that students involved in activities actually do better in school. Those who have a full schedule tend to do a better job of managing their time—they have to. People with less to do tend to procrastinate, resulting in poorer grades. Get involved! You won't regret it.

CHAPTER 13

Working in School

Late weekday nights, my friend Meredith often finds herself mopping floors, counting money (not her own, of course), making popcorn, and kneeling on sticky surfaces to pick up strangers' candy wrappers. She works at a movie theater and, after work, she knows she has to go home and finish her term paper and read 50 pages of her European history textbook. Yet she still says with a smile, "It was here that I saw my first double feature of Reservoir Dogs *and* Pulp Fiction. *The screen had scratches and the sound was really bad, but it convinced me that if I'd ever do a movie, I would show it on that screen first." She is planning to work in the film industry after college, and in a strange way, her present job is education for the future and serves as the first step toward her vision.*

After talking with Meredith, I decided to apply for a job at a one-hour photo-processing store, hoping that I would find the same joy she had discovered in involving my hands in something I loved: photography. That didn't work, though, and soon after landing the job I quit in an emotional outburst of frustration. I hated developing other people's summer vacation photos, knowing that I could be out shooting my own and doing better, grander things with the time that I was spending behind those counters.

> *The ever-present stench of chemicals began to sting my eyes and follow me like a shadow, acting as a constant reminder of the hours I'd be spending at work on that Friday night while the rest of my friends were out at coffee shops, laughing and listening to some beatific mod-band. I complained excessively. I could no longer be the perky salesperson that my paycheck expected me to be.*
>
> *I would get home from work and attempt to entertain my late nights with sitcoms, infomercials, or anything that would be a diversion, but even then my body would simply give out and early the next morning I would find myself with yesterday's dinner on my face—my dog licking its remains—and an inexplicable addiction to* Melrose Place.
>
> —ORLANDO, SAN DEGUITO ACADEMY, ENCINITAS, CALIFORNIA

Often, teenagers will work long and strenuous hours at minimum wage for a couple of bucks and a glimmer of hope that they will gain some sense of satisfaction from the hours that they spend greeting customers. Businesses, usually in the retail and food industries, hire young people because they know that we are willing to work, even if it means building up a sweat and getting our hands dirty.

Of course, not everyone chooses to work during high school, but if you do decide to take on a job, you still have a few more choices to make—and these choices can make the difference between making your job a meaningful addition to your high school experience or letting it turn into a hellish ordeal.

As with any decision, the choice to take on a job—and what kind of job to take—should be an informed one. We hope this list of tips will make having a job in high school a bit less hectic and a bit more gratifying.

> *I started working for three main reasons. One was that my friends were all working as busboys, and there was a job opening in the same restaurant. Another was that my parents had been constantly urging me to get a job and save for college. And, lastly, the speeding tickets I had to pay were definitely a consideration. So I went and got an interview and was hired soon after. I knew that I would be earning money, but I didn't know that it would be such hard work; I come home exhausted every Saturday night, smelling like a kitchen. But I also didn't know that it would be so much fun; I meet new people every day, and the guys I work with have become really good friends. I have definitely learned a lot—and I am going to keep the job even after I pay off those tickets.*
>
> —PETER, HERITAGE HIGH SCHOOL, LITTLETON, COLORADO

JOB BASICS

1. VOLUNTEER BEFORE YOU GET A JOB.

Volunteering for a local charity or a soup kitchen gives you an opportunity to get a sense of what working is like, but in a less stressful environment. You can schedule your hours to fit your own lifestyle, and you will probably find that volunteer work is a more rewarding than a real job. It is extremely easy to find volunteering opportunities (see Chapter 14, "Community Service")—the problem is no money! If you need to save for college, support your family, supplement your allowance, or satisfy your addiction to music CDs, volunteering may not be your best option. Still, volunteering does spiff up your resume for future employers (they like work experience, which includes volunteer jobs) and college applications.

2. Have a reason for working.

Don't just get a job because you think it would be cool to have a little extra cash. If you need extra money for ski equipment or for your college savings, then you might want to get a job, but you should know why you're working. Usually students who just decide to work for the heck of it end up not having the commitment necessary to hold down the job. Set goals for yourself and have a purpose in mind, whether that includes saving for college or a spring break trip, or paying off that money that you owe your older brother.

> *Because of my car accident I had to work and pay. But I ended up loving my job at the bagel shop. We would have bagel fights, and on my last day we turned up the background music really loud because George Michael was on. It was a really cool job, and between cleaning and slicing bagels, we managed to have a lot of fun.*
>
> —Danielle, San Deguito Academy, Encinitas, California

3. Be ready to get down and dirty.

Okay, let's face it. The job market for teens isn't as expansive and full of options as we wish it was. You can skip right over those classified ads for "Administrative Assistant"—unless we're talking an administrative assistant at the local burger joint. And you'll probably have a hard time beating out the other candidates for the clerical position at that hip fashion magazine downtown. No, for us there lies a common fate: ending up behind a counter murmuring that ever-so-classic question, "Would you like fries with that?" Okay, so once you have gotten over any romantic visions of secretaries and power ties, then you can begin to think realistically about the kinds of jobs that you might be able to find.

Be prepared to lift heavy boxes, be prepared to make best friends with a mop, and be prepared to have to smile and nod to managers who are no more excited about their line of work than you are. Even if you work at a clothing store or a video rental shop, where you'd expect a laid-back atmosphere, the odd tasks that no one wants to do will without a doubt be handed over to the new person, especially if you're a teenager. You can avoid disappointment by not expecting royal treatment at your first job.

4. BE AWARE THAT YOUR SOCIAL LIFE COULD BE SHOT.

Realize what you are getting into before you make a commitment to a job. You know who you are, and if you rely on your time with friends to maintain your sanity, you might want to think closely about forfeiting friend-time for work-time. There is probably some way to organize your time so that you can accommodate work, school, and friends in your schedule, but be sure you think about just how that can happen before you sign up to work a few eight-hour shifts. In this case, cutting your spending habits may be a better option than joining the local workforce.

Of course, having a job actually can help out in the social scene, too. Chances are that you will make new friends at work. Often, your coworkers will be different ages and will have different backgrounds than the people you know at school. Also, having a little extra money in your pocket is always helpful when you and your friends decide to catch that awesome concert.

5. WORK SOMEWHERE WHERE YOU FEEL COMFORTABLE.

Work environment should be a key consideration when choosing a job. You should think about where you would like to work before filling out a stack of applications. If you get headaches easily, then that loud restaurant down the street is probably not right. If you are a vegetarian and the sight of meat makes you sick, then you can probably rule out McDonald's pretty quick. If, on the other hand, you're the type that needs a fast pace and busy atmosphere to stay energized, then a bookstore is not for you.

Another way to find a place where you feel comfortable working is to think about your personal interests before you go job searching. If you are interested in working in government, then you might call the county courthouse to see if they need any part-time help, or you might put up a sign at the courthouse offering to do clerical work in a law office. Finding work in an area of interest is always a great plus. Be aggressive in trying to find the appropriate workplace for you and your temperament.

6. ESTABLISH A GOOD RAPPORT WITH PEOPLE AT WORK.

Be honest from the start with your manager, and make sure that he or she knows about the shifts and the number of hours that you will be able to work. Most people who have employed high school students in the past are willing to accommodate a high schooler's schedule. You can make these situations less uncomfortable by making your limits clear to your manager up front from the start.

You will also want to develop positive relationships with your manager and your coworkers so that when the inevitable crisis arises, someone there will be willing to reorganize your schedule or cover your shift.

If you have a positive attitude, show up on time, and work hard, chances are that any manager will be understanding when you ask for a lighter load one week so that you can study for your physics final.

> *Sometimes I can do my homework at work when things aren't too busy. My boss is very cool, and he usually lets me do homework because he knows that school is very important to me. Although it can be difficult sometimes, now that I have a job I've realized that there is only so much I can do in a day.*
>
> —CRISTINA, TRUCKEE HIGH SCHOOL, TRUCKEE, CALIFORNIA

7. DON'T GET PRESSURED INTO THINGS.

Sometimes a manager will try to take advantage of your position by trying to pressure you to take more hours than you have requested. It's okay to be firm and say no (politely, of course). If this doesn't work, blame it on your school counselor or your parents—say something like, "I'm really sorry but my parents have said that I'm not allowed to work more than two shifts per week."

Also don't fall for the trap of being offered a pseudo-promotion. Sometimes managers will promote you to some kind of made-up position such as "shift captain" or "assistant manager," and as soon as you accept the promotion and the 10-cent raise that accompanies it, they tell you that you have to work a minimum of 30 hours a week and that you have just accepted a whole host of new responsibilities. This is not the case with all promotions, but the next time someone asks, "How would you like to be an assistant manager?" you might want to respond with, "What exactly does that entail?" before answering yes.

8. Know the employment regulations in your state.

Although work regulations for minors vary from state to state, you can talk to your school guidance counselor about any important applicable laws in your state. In many states, you must fill out a work permit before beginning to work. On the back of the permit, the regulations are spelled out, stating how many hours each age category can work and listing other rules regarding the consequences if work affects your education negatively. If you have other questions, you can contact the U.S. Department of Labor office in your state.

9. Remember your priorities.

Do not sacrifice school for your job. In the long run, school pays off. If you notice that your GPA is slipping and that your schedule is overwhelming, consider cutting back on your work schedule. Your high school grades go on your permanent record and are important for college admissions; your high school job is probably temporary.

10. It's a job, not a life.

Juggling a job with all your other activities and school work is difficult, and a successful balance will involve some give and take. But don't get too stressed: If your job and school combined are turning you into a nervous wreck, make some changes in your schedule. Your high school years are not supposed to be the most stressful in your life. Make sure you have some time to play.

Knowing When to Get Out . . .

The best part about having a job in high school is that, unlike school itself, you can quit your job. But don't just quit on a whim. If you are unhappy, talk to your parents or your guidance counselor. It's okay to quit when the job isn't a good match, but you should make an effort to *make* it a good match. Also talk to your manager if you are unhappy; you may be surprised at how receptive he or she is to your problems. If you decide you want to get out, give your notice (two weeks is pretty standard for a part-time job) and look elsewhere for something that will be more manageable and more enjoyable.

CHAPTER 14

Community Service

For my freshman history class, we were required to research a problem in our society and then do a service project about it. I chose eating disorders as my area of concern. I learned so much about a problem that so few understand, and I got to speak with some girls who had survived the disease. As my service project, I went to a middle school and spoke about eating disorders to them, educating them as I wish everyone would be. I didn't imagine that it could be so rewarding: I learned a ton and now understand so much more about how some teenagers think—and that has helped me direct my own life. That's not to mention how much fun it was getting to meet some really cool people and then share my own experiences—it was definitely worth missing my favorite TV program."

—MERRITT, HERITAGE HIGH SCHOOL, LITTLETON, COLORADO

No one ever told me how hard senior year was going to be. Now that I'm in my final year, I've found myself turning into one big ball of stress. With college application deadlines fast approaching, just thinking about all those personal essays makes me want to reconsider spending another year in high school.

—MEREDITH, MERCER ISLAND HIGH SCHOOL, MERCER ISLAND, WASHINGTON

Okay, so maybe that's a little extreme. But it can be pretty overwhelming to look at the college application forms and see all the little boxes that need to be filled with grades, activities, sports, and even *community service*. Some college applications have full sections dedicated to your participation (or non-participation) in volunteer work. Not only do they want to see that you were active and productive during your high school years, but they also want to know that you've made contributions outside of the classroom.

Of course, there are more important reasons to participate in community service than college applications. Community service is your way of showing your appreciation and gratitude for the things that you have, and it's a way for you to share your talents with others who may not be as fortunate.

WHERE TO START? FINDING THE RIGHT ACTIVITY FOR YOU

With all the volunteer opportunities available, you might have trouble figuring out where to begin. Fortunately, with a few tips, you can get a head start on your community service work and be sure that when college application time comes, you'll have more than enough to say.

1. GET INVOLVED EARLY.

Start getting involved in community service and volunteer work during your freshman year. You'll give yourself plenty of time to try out different types of community service activities and find something that you enjoy and that suits your interests. If you discover that you really like helping out at the local food bank or tutoring elementary school students, then you've got four more years to spend doing something worthwhile and even fun.

Most students get through the first three years of high school without doing any community service. By the time they become seniors, however, they send themselves into volunteer overdrive as they try to make up for lost time and rack up an impressive list of credentials for college admissions officers. Unfortunately for them, colleges want to see that they have been balancing their work over four years. They're not looking for the student who spends two hours walking the neighbor's dog during sophomore year and then senior year dividing time between six different charities. Colleges want people with a demonstrated and enduring sense of commitment to helping others.

2. USE ALL YOUR AVAILABLE RESOURCES TO FIND COMMUNITY SERVICE WORK.

Most likely, you have plenty of information about volunteer opportunities right at your fingertips—literally. Just head to your computer and use the Internet to either check up on local organizations or to get an idea of what kind of work is out there. If you don't have access to the Internet, you still have many other available sources for information. Most likely, your schools have pamphlets or brochures about local service organizations. Maybe your school even runs its own community service club. If you're involved in any religious youth groups, there are probably affiliated activities in which you can participate. Also ask a school counselor: He or she should know where to look.

When you hear about something that interests you, try it out. Maybe you'll find that your arms just weren't cut out for an activity as rigorous as scrubbing away at stubborn graffiti. But finding out what you *don't* like is almost as good as finding out what you *do* like: It narrows your options.

If you're having trouble getting started, don't be afraid to ask around. Big organizations aren't the only places looking for your help. You'll almost always find that you can come in handy to the elderly couple down the street or the local nursing home or YMCA. You'll be surprised at what you can find if you just ask—and if you're free.

3. GET INVOLVED IN SOMETHING YOU ENJOY.

Don't do community service work you hate. There's nothing worse than involuntary volunteering. Not only do you put yourself through misery, but you also miss the point of community service: willingly spending your time and talents helping others. If you can't stand getting yourself dirty or you don't like animals, then why waste your time cleaning out messy pig pens at the county fair? When you offer to take part in a service activity, you're offering to sacrifice a portion of your time; make the time worth it.

If you're thinking of going into a health profession, maybe you'd rather spend your time at a hospital. Or, if you'd like to be a teacher, tutoring might be more rewarding.

4. CAN'T FIND IT? START IT UP!

What if you're really interested in building playground equipment for the neighborhood kids, but you can't find an organization that will help you? Start your own service group! Talk to your friends, parents, teachers, and community leaders about your idea. Chances are, you'll get plenty of encouragement and support. By tailoring your work to fit your interests and personality, you'll find that community service can be a lot of fun.

5. KNOW WHAT YOU'RE GETTING INTO FROM THE START.

When your community center's annual holiday festival committee coaxed you into agreeing to provide entertainment, did that mean that they were expecting you to call around for a local magician or puppeteering troupe, or did that mean that they were counting on you to be the entertainment? If you know what you are getting into from the very beginning, you will save yourself confusion and avoid having to spend hours honing your juggling skills and balloon-twisting techniques. Before you sign up to do anything, ask questions such as these:

- Who will be working with you?

- How should you go about doing the work?

- What kinds of jobs will you be asked to do?

- How much time is expected of you?

Don't commit to doing an activity if you're not sure what it entails. You probably will not be too happy if you wind up having far more work than you expected, or if you end up with hardly any responsibilities at all. However, if you have already committed yourself to a service job and can't find a good way to get out of doing it, try to look for the positive in it.

> *Last year, I spent a lot of time volunteering at a hospital. I didn't really like it very much because I was given a lot of extra work that I didn't expect to be doing—stuff that I was given to do because there was nothing else for me to do. There was one thing that I thought was kind of cool about the job, though. There were these canisters, just like at bank drive-throughs, that I could put messages inside and send through one of those delivery tubes. That sometimes helped make the job more fun.*
>
> —RACHEL, WALLA WALLA, WASHINGTON

6. LOOK FOR OPPORTUNITIES AT SCHOOL.

Your school may have classes or service organizations that you can join. Many schools offer tutoring programs, run food and clothing drives, and support activities within the community. You'd be amazed at how much more enjoyable school is when you take part in service clubs and activities. Not only will you make plenty of new friends (with similar interests) and gain newfound respect from peers and teachers, but you may develop more confidence and perhaps even some leadership skills.

7. LOOK BEYOND YOUR IMMEDIATE COMMUNITY.

You might not always find the right service activities in your own neighborhood or community. If that is the case, look beyond your immediate resources. Maybe you live in a sheltered suburb but would like to volunteer in the city at a homeless shelter. Or, if you live in a crowded metropolis, maybe you'd prefer helping to plant trees in a nearby town. Becoming involved in community service does not limit you to your own community. In fact, helping out in other communities is a great way for you to meet new people and become exposed to different cultures and ways of life. Remember when you thought that everyone used the word *soda* and were shocked to hear that others called it *pop* (or vice versa)? Well, it's kind of the same when you volunteer outside your community. You'll find that even though there might be many differences between yourself and the people you're helping, you also will have plenty in common.

> *During the spring of 1998, my church youth group from Seattle went on a mission trip across the state to a sister church in a poorer rural area. A lot of the families had young kids and were struggling just to be able to have the basics in life, so their church didn't have a lot of extra money. One of the things their church needed was a place for all the kids to play, especially since the church was a really important part of their lives. Our youth group was to build a playground: We dug tether-ball pits, set up a volleyball pit, and set up some huge tires for the kids to play on. I went into the trip expecting it to be pretty boring and expecting to go to a place where the people really didn't need help. But when I got there, I realized that we really could help them. There were a lot of little kids who deserved to have more than they had. I came away from the trip with a better understanding that life isn't always easy and that I often take things for granted. The trip was rewarding because it gave me a different outlook on life. Not only did I experience a different environment, but I also met a lot of people I would never have met otherwise.*
>
> —LINDSAY, MERCER ISLAND HIGH SCHOOL, MERCER ISLAND, WASHINGTON

8. DON'T PUT YOURSELF IN A BIND.

Manage your time well. You're the one who is going to have to balance community service with school, sports, music lessons, church, family, friends, free time, dating, and other activities. The demands on your time can often be overwhelming.

When you sign up for a community service activity, be reasonable. Do you really want to spend three hours at the nursing home every day after soccer practice, even if it means that you won't be able to finish your homework until 2 a.m.? Sure, you might enjoy singing karaoke with the elderly, but at the rate you're going, you'll wear yourself out before second semester—and chances are that you won't even make it through the whole Bing Crosby collection. Although you may have made a commitment to be at the nursing home every day, you also have a commitment to your schoolwork, your health, and keeping up with the other activities you enjoy. Don't take on more than you can handle; it's not fair to you or to the people who are depending on you to perform at your best.

9. BE COMMITTED.

Still, if you make a firm commitment to a community service organization or project, you are responsible for maintaining that commitment. If you say that you will be at the food bank every Sunday evening at 5:00, be there. You wouldn't tell your boss at Baskin-Robbins that you will be at work after school and then not show up. Even though you don't get money for community service, it's still a job, so treat it as such. If you come down with the flu and are unable to hand out food on Sunday, call ahead of time and let someone know. If you find that you are consistently having to call in to say you won't be there, rearrange your volunteer times to better fit your schedule. The people you're helping have chosen you because you are responsible and eager to become involved with them, and they depend on you. Don't let them down.

10. ATTITUDE AND EFFORT COUNT MORE THAN TIME.

Unless you're superhuman—or just superorganized—you probably will not be able to spend any more than a few hours a week doing community service. School, homework, eating, and sleeping alone consume practically three-fourths of your time, and you still want to have time for sports and other extracurricular activities (and maybe even some TV and movies). If you can only spend two hours a week playing foosball and air hockey with the kids at your community center, then that's great. If you can spend more than a few hours with all those rowdy kids, then that's even better. More important than the time you spend is your attitude and effort. Be positive. Don't feel like you're doing anyone a favor. Community service is supposed to be as rewarding for you as for the people you are serving.

11. GET YOUR FRIENDS INVOLVED.

If you're anything like the average high school student, you enjoy spending time with your friends. So why not take them along when you do your volunteer work? Not only will your friends appreciate the opportunity to try something new, but the organization you're helping will be ecstatic that you've recruited extra help. Friends also can make your work more enjoyable—and when you're having fun, it is easy to forget just how hard you are working. Don't invite your goof-off friends, though. The idea is to help the organization, not destroy it or cause problems. Gather up friends who you know will do a good job, like you.

12. TAKE ADVANTAGE OF SUMMER OPPORTUNITIES.

Most likely, your school year will be filled with so many activities that you won't be able to find too much time to become really involved in service work. If the school year is too busy, take advantage of summer. This is the best time to volunteer and do community service because you have plenty of extra hours to spare, even if you have a job.

Different types of volunteer jobs may be available during the summer. For example, you can spend two months as a counselor at your favorite childhood camp, or you can join that three-week mission trip to Mexico. Some of your friends may spend their whole summer vegging out at home and watching old '80s movies on TBS. This may sound relaxing to you after you've suffered through your second-semester finals, but in September you'll hear a lot of them complaining and wishing that your friends had actually done something over the summer.

13. KEEP TRACK OF WHAT YOU'RE DOING.

When you're filling out your college or work applications, you don't want to be spending hours trying to remember what you were doing the second week of July after your freshman year. Every little bit of work counts, and the strength of your resume should not be diminished because you were unable to remember all your activities. You deserve credit for all your hard work.

14. But at the same time, remember what's important. . . .

Hopefully, college applications are not the only reason you're doing community service. When your dream school does accept you, are you suddenly going to stop caring about others and doing what you can to help them? Community service is more than just a step toward college. The confidence and insight you will gain from working with and helping others are qualities that will be valuable for the rest of your life. Service activities will help you to develop a better understanding of different types of people. Nothing else you can do will give you the satisfaction of teaching a less able student how to read, or painting a new community center that will be used by everyone in your area, or handing out food to those who are needy.

Get Out and Make a Difference!

The responsibilities of involvement in community service are similar to holding down a job, except the rewards are different. You don't get a paycheck, but volunteer work pays you in a different way. To begin with, you can make yourself more appealing to the college of your choice. More importantly, service activities will give you a greater understanding of yourself and others. The life lessons you learn, combined with the gratitude and respect of the people you help, often make for experiences and memories more valuable than money could ever buy.

CHAPTER 15

Friends

> *I thought my middle school friends were cool, but in high school I met people who were true kindred spirits. I have met some of the most amazing people and had so much fun. I think friends are one of the most valuable and important aspects of your life—especially in high school, when everything can get so confusing. It is so awesome to know that you can always trust your friends to be there for you.*
>
> —MERRITT, HERITAGE HIGH SCHOOL, LITTLETON, COLORADO

High school is an amazing time in your life when you will be given more freedom and responsibility. It is also a time when you will form strong friendships that may last for the rest of your life. Your true friends will be there for you when you need them, and they will make each experience a little better. You can laugh with them, cry with them, and share your experiences together. But friendships, especially in high school, are not easy. Following are some tips to help you form and maintain friendships—the right kind of friendships—in high school.

15 TIPS ON FRIENDSHIPS

1. REACH OUT AND ACTIVELY TRY TO MEET NEW FRIENDS.

High school is an incredible opportunity to make new friends and meet many interesting people. Your previous friends from middle school may change in high school because you probably won't have the same people

in all your classes. Although it might be difficult if your group of friends changes, meeting new people is exciting. Some good ways to find new friends are to join sports teams or after-school clubs, where you will find a variety of students that you have probably never talked to before and who are interested in similar activities. Don't be afraid to chat with new people you meet and try to appear open and approachable. Remember that the other people in your grade are in the same boat, and they all want to make some new friends just like you do.

2. TRY TO BE FRIENDS WITH MANY DIFFERENT TYPES OF PEOPLE.

Once you enter high school, you will have the chance to get to know many different students. Be friendly with everyone, at least at first. You never know if the person sitting behind you in chemistry could one day turn out to be a good friend or, at the very least, help you with an assignment. If you try to talk to many different students, you will be able to meet people with a variety of interests.

3. DON'T BE AFRAID TO BEFRIEND PEOPLE WHO ARE DIFFERENT THAN YOUR USUAL SET OF FRIENDS.

Don't decide that you won't be friends with the guy sitting next to you just because he is wearing different clothes or speaking a different language. Part of high school is learning how to socialize with people who are different than you. It's hard to assess people based solely on how they look. The guy speaking a different language may turn out to be the best soccer player in school. Of course, after an initial chat you may decide not to befriend someone, which is perfectly acceptable. You can't (and won't) be friends with everyone, but give people a chance.

4. DON'T SECLUDE YOURSELF IN ONE CLIQUE OF FRIENDS.

Although it is great to have a few really close friends, it is also important to try to be inclusive. You never know if your small group of friends might suddenly break apart. If you only talk to and spend time with the same people, then you won't have others to turn to if your friendships start to change. Cliques have a reputation for being harsh and deciding that one member of the clique does not fit in anymore. If you are the one who does not fit in anymore, you'll be glad you made some other acquaintances.

5. Surround yourself with people who accept you and treat you well.

Spend time with people who appreciate you and accept you for who you are. That might sound stupid, but many people choose friends who belittle them and make them feel terrible about themselves. If you feel like you have to put on an act when you're around certain people, then you probably are not a good match. If a select group of students doesn't respect you, then these people do not deserve you as a friend.

Make sure that you feel comfortable and secure around the people with whom you spend time. You should not hesitate to say and act the way you really feel when you are around your friends. If you are always dreading to hang out with a specific individual because he or she does not treat you well, then he or she probably isn't a good friend. Find other people who you feel comfortable with and who appreciate your good qualities.

6. Be true to yourself.

Friends are often a great place to turn to when you need advice. They can give you their own opinion and offer you a different point of view. However, you should not model all your thoughts and actions after your friends. Make sure you are true to what you believe in and that you value your own opinion, not just what your friends think. Friends can be a great source of advice and fun, but they should not take over your life and your personality. You will note that some of your old friends will change completely to suit others in high school. Be careful not to fall into that trap.

7. Move on from friendships that are causing you grief.

Some friendships won't last forever, or even past the first year of high school. But don't end friendships after one fight. Communication is crucial. After you have had some time to calm down, talk with your friend about why you are upset. Most times you will work it out and forget why you were fighting in the first place. Some friendships, though, are not meant to be. If a particular friend makes you feel like trash every time you talk or is not happy when good things happen for you, you might want to call it quits. Ending a friendship is not easy, and there's no right or wrong way to do it. Sometimes it just happens without anyone saying anything. After some time apart, there is a good chance that you will become better friends again later. Hanging out with other people may make you appreciate each other more.

8. Don't let your friends pressure you.

True friends will never force you to do something that is harmful or that will make you feel terribly uncomfortable. If they care about you, they will look out for you and help you, not try to pressure you into something that you don't want to do. Make what you value clear from the beginning of a friendship. If your friends can't accept your decisions, then talk to them about respecting your choices. Feel free to say no. If they still don't understand, consider looking for some other friends. High school will be (and should be) a time for many crazy and hilarious adventures. Don't let your friends ruin this experience by trying to force you to be become involved in dangerous experiences that do not interest you.

> One time, my friends and I were going to a concert, and all my friends were smoking pot and I really didn't want to. So I told them, and they pressured me into it. When I woke up the next morning—passed out at my friend's house—I felt so used. Since then, I have tried to find some new people to hang out with because that incident made me realize that those people weren't my real friends. They couldn't accept me, and so I couldn't accept myself. Now I am much more confident, and I am so much happier when I am with friends who respect my decisions.
>
> —John, Little Rock, Arkansas

9. Keep their secrets.

One of the greatest aspects of friendships is the opportunity to grow close enough with your friends to feel comfortable sharing very personal things. You know how important it is for you to trust someone before you are able to open up to them. That's because trust is crucial in maintaining friendships. If someone tells you something confidential, you need to respect this information and keep it to yourself. If you slip up and spill the secret, your friend may never feel comfortable opening up to you again. Trust is one of the hardest things to rebuild, so make sure that you prove yourself trustworthy. If you are bad at keeping secrets, don't encourage people to tell you stuff that they want kept secret.

> *One summer I was really bummed about not getting into camp, so I wrote my friend a letter telling her how I knew that other people got in even though I was supposedly first on the wait list. She shared the letter with her whole cabin, and eventually her counselors saw the letter. Her counselors told the camp director, and she got really mad at me for what she called my "guilt-trip letter." I didn't mean for it to be like that at all. I was just sort of venting, and I felt so betrayed that my friend shared my private thoughts with everyone. I still can't trust her enough to tell her secrets.*
>
> —MERRITT, HERITAGE HIGH SCHOOL, LITTLETON, COLORADO

An important aside: If your friend's safety or health depends on you divulging a secret, do it. For example, if your friend confides in you that she is making herself throw up after she eats, you should not keep this to yourself. Eating disorders can be life threatening, and it is important that you talk to your parents or another trusted adult to help your friend. Use good judgment and don't divulge secrets on a whim. But it is worth the risk of losing your friend's trust to save him or her from possible injury or death. Your friend will thank you later.

10. DON'T TALK BEHIND YOUR FRIENDS' BACKS.

Remember the old saying, "Whatever goes around comes around." This rule definitely applies to friendships. If you talk negatively about your friends behind their backs, eventually they will hear about it. It may seem innocent if one day you are just sitting at lunch making negative comments about your friends. But if they find out, they will probably be very hurt and angry, and you will have a lot of explaining to do. We all know how upsetting it is to hear that someone else was talking about you behind your back. Being funny or making a joke at the expense of a friend is probably not worth it.

11. Be supportive of your friends.

High school is a time of laughter and fun, but there also will be some difficult times. Support your friends through challenging and trying situations. You may have a friend who just lost a parent or grandparent. One of your friends may find out that he was not accepted into his first-choice college. Your best friend may have just gotten dumped by her boyfriend. Being comforting and considerate may simply mean giving a friend a hug when you see him or her. Ask your friends how they are doing, too; some of their problems may seem trivial to you, but they're not to them. Your friends might not have many other people they feel comfortable turning to, so your presence and reassuring words are important. If you are there for your friends in hard times, then they will do the same for you when you need help.

12. Give more than you take.

The best friends are the ones who give more than they take. They are the ones who bring you notes from class when you are sick or help you put up posters if you are running for student government. If both sides of a friendship are giving more than taking, the result is usually a pretty strong friendship.

13. Listen. Listen. Listen.

The ability to listen is one of the most important qualities in a friend. Good listeners usually have more true friends than good talkers, even if it doesn't always seem that way. Practice being a good listener. Listen closely. Repeat back to the person what you think he or she is saying so your friend knows that you are listening. Be interested.

Mike called me that night. He asked if he could just talk to me. I told him I had to study for a big test, and I would maybe catch a minute tomorrow. Even when he just asked for five minutes, I said that I would call him when I was done with my homework. He called three other people before he shot himself that night. I always think, "If only I had given him a couple minutes just to listen. . . ."

　　　　　　　　　　　　　　　　　　　　　—ANONYMOUS

If your friend confides in you about a problem, don't interrupt to tell him or her what *you* think or that he or she is wrong for feeling a certain way. Try not to judge or critique what your friend is saying. It is important that you listen with an open ear to understand what your friend is feeling. Let's say that your friend, Tracy, tells you that her parents are getting a divorce and that she is really upset about it. Give her the opportunity to explain her emotions, even though it may be difficult to hear her complain about her anger or sadness. Your help may be the only thing that gets her through that tough time. Just giving your friend a shoulder to cry on is often enough to help.

14. DON'T FORGET ABOUT YOUR FRIENDS IF YOU HAVE A BOYFRIEND OR GIRLFRIEND.

Don't drop your friends the minute Mr. Studly or Ms. America walks into your life. Make sure that you save some time to spend with your friends as well as with your boyfriend or girlfriend. Marrying your high school sweetheart is unlikely; good friendships most often last longer than hot romances. The key here is balance. If your new boyfriend tells you that you have to spend all your time with him, he is probably not the right guy. If you feel like spending all your time with your new girlfriend, try to give yourself—and her—a little space for some other friends.

15. FIGHT FAIR.

Although friendships are usually full of happiness and fun, expect to engage in an occasional fight with your friends. The way you deal with these sticky situations may determine how long your friendships will last. If you find yourself arguing with friends, stay calm and try not to use underhanded tactics, such as telling everyone that your friend is a slut or trying to break up your friend's relationship. Screaming is usually not as productive as straightforward talk. Be willing to admit when you're wrong, and don't be too proud to 'fess up if you've made a mistake. Sometimes the best thing that a friend can hear is that you are sorry. If you apologize when you mess up, it will be much easier for your friend to do the same.

CHAPTER 16

Dating in High School

> *Dating makes high school relationships totally different. Even though it can be really fun, it is also kind of bad because now if you talk to a guy, everyone labels it "flirting," and assumes that you're interested that way. In middle school, you could actually just talk to guys, but once you hit high school, you're automatically rated as date material.*
>
> —MERRITT, HERITAGE HIGH SCHOOL, LITTLETON, COLORADO

Are you "going out" with him? This may be one of the most confusing questions you will ever face, and the truth is that almost everyone has faced the question more than once. To be "going out" with someone is such a familiar term, yet its interpretations vary more than those of the Bible. People's interpretation of this term seems to change as they grow older, too. Once in high school people may begin to say that someone is "dating" rather than "going out," but in the end both phrases are so vague that they can mean anything. Well, whatever you or your friends choose to call it, dating in high school can be a lot of fun—and, at times, not so much fun.

The goal of this chapter is to provide some useful tips, stories, and ideas to make dating in high school less stressful and maybe even more enjoyable. But books like this one can tell you only so much. Most of what you learn about dating will come from your own experiences (in high school and beyond) and the ups and downs that make dating such a funny, interesting, and important part of people's lives.

Many students never go on a date in high school. In fact, many of the authors of this book have never been on a date. If you have not been on a date, don't worry: You are not alone. You can still read this chapter if you are interested in the topic, or you can save it for college. Dating is not a necessity in high school. We just thought it would be fun to include dating and some dating tips as a chapter for those who are dating or planning on asking someone out at some point in the future.

ASKING SOMEONE OUT

Asking someone out on a date is the hardest part of dating. It's stressful. It can be embarrassing. It can be downright humiliating. Here are some thoughts to help ease the anxiety if you are thinking about asking someone on a date.

GROUP DATES ARE LESS INTIMATE THAN ONE-ON-ONE ADVENTURES

The first decision you need to make is whether the date will be a group date with friends or a single date, with just you and your date. Group dates are obviously less intimate, which can be a plus—especially if you're a bit nervous. If you go on a group date, it'll be a lot easier to ask the person, because both you and your date will feel more comfortable with friends around.

Group dates can be especially good if you and your date don't know each other very well. If the thought of a one-on-one date with just you and your partner scares you, then a group date will be less pressure-filled. One-on-one dates also are great once you know someone reasonably well.

GET TO KNOW THE PERSON BEFORE YOUR DATE

Get to know the person a little before you commit a whole night to a date. Getting to know a person includes talking on the phone or talking at school. The better you know each other, the less likely it is that you will feel weird when it's just the two of you, or the two of you in small group. Okay, so your first goal should be to talk on the phone without having to plan what you're going to say. If you can talk on the phone or in person, then you'll probably manage more than nervous monosyllabic answers throughout the date.

THE ONLY THING YOU HAVE TO FEAR IS FEAR ITSELF

One of the most common reasons that people have for not asking someone out on a date is the fear of being rejected. The truth is that if you can't get up the courage to ask someone out, then you better not expect to do much dating. Yeah, he or she might say no, but it's far more likely that your prospect will say yes. You might as well give it a try—have confidence in yourself.

> *I am a really shy person naturally, so when it came to dealing with girls, I could barely look them in the eye. Until a couple months ago, I figured, "The heck with it! I'm gonna go for her!" So I asked my crush out, and she said yes. Since then, I've been a lot more courageous—and it's definitely been worth it. I've had a lot of fun with people I might have been too shy to ask out before. My advice: Go for it. If you don't, you'll always think, "What if?. . ."*
>
> —PHIL, HERITAGE HIGH SCHOOL, LITTLETON, COLORADO

GIRLS, THIS IS THE NEW MILLENNIUM

Don't forget that girls can do the asking, too. Actually, many guys prefer for a girl to do the asking because it takes the pressure off. It's true that guys generally do more asking than girls, but there is no reason to be old-fashioned. Many guys often suffer from fear of rejection and therefore can't get themselves to ask out anyone. Guys love it when the girls help them out. If you both just sit around waiting for the other one to ask, then maybe you'll never go out!

MAKE THE CALL

Whether you want to do a group date or a one-on-one affair, you've got to make the call to ask out the person. Remember, you don't have to talk for too long. We've all had conversations with a crush that sound something like this:

You: "Hi, this is Sarah, how are you?"

Crush: "Fine, what's up?"

You: "Not much, what's going on"

Crush: "Um . . . yeah . . . so . . . ."

To avoid such conversations, just tell yourself that after you exchange the obligatory greeting—"Hey, what's up?"—and after your potential date responds, simply say, "I was wondering whether you might like to go out on Friday." Chances are, if he or she says yes, you may have to control the urge to scream "Yes!" If you are becoming nervous and have nothing else to say, just end the conversation with: "Great, well, I'll call you later this week to make plans."

Of course, if the person says "No," he or she will probably offer some kind of excuse. You should listen carefully to this excuse because later in the evening you and several of your friends will likely spend a couple hours analyzing each word. Did he really have other plans? If he did, does this mean that he wants me to call again? Could she possibly be trimming her poodle on Friday night? (By the way, very few people trim poodles on Friday night.)

If you get someone who offers a really lame excuse—for example, "I'm sorry, I have to rewind my CDs"—then it may be time to move on. There are other fish in the sea.

WHEN YOU ARE OUT ON THE TOWN

The most important thing to remember when you're actually out on a first date is to be yourself. If you try to be someone else, you will just look foolish. Plus, if you're going to start any kind of relationship, you want it to be based on reality, not on lousy acting. So relax, or at least try not to be too jittery, and be yourself.

DON'T BE EARLY, DON'T BE LATE

A few minutes after the scheduled time is "fashionably late" for a first date; 15 minutes is late, not fashionably late. Of course, if you are meeting somewhere, you should be there on time—there is no such thing as fashionably late when you're meeting at the food court of the local shopping mall. Don't go early to someone's house, either: Everyone wants his or her fully allotted time to get ready for a first date.

STAY AWAY FROM MESSY FOODS

On your first date with someone, you'll probably want to go for the chicken breast over the baby-back ribs smothered in BBQ sauce. When the menu comes, however, remember that you are nervous and should not order anything that requires great amounts of coordination to eat. Stay away from foods that you might easily end up wearing.

Girls, guys feel stupid when you order a "side salad, with dressing on the side" as your main course. Guys, girls hate it when you make snide comments about how much or how little they are eating. Remember, you want your date to be comfortable, too.

WHO SHOULD PAY?

For some reason, who should pay is always an awkward question. The answer is go with your gut instinct. The best bet is probably to offer to split things down the middle. Alternatively, it might be easier to have one person pay for dinner and the other pay for a movie. Of course, if you are really having a great time and know that you will want to go for another date, then when it comes time to pay, you can insist on taking the check and say, "You can get it next time." Ah, the perfect set-up.

Don't make a big deal out of who's paying. If your date absolutely insists on paying, then just say, "Thank you very much." Don't spend the rest of the evening trying to sneak money into his shirt pocket or her purse.

SAY THANK YOU

Whether or not you intend to date the person again, you should always thank him or her before calling it a night. A sincere thank-you will either set the tone for a new relationship or be a nice way to end an evening that probably won't be repeated.

When Your Date Is Not the Same Age as You

If during your freshman year you found out that your parents bugged your phone line and went through your room everyday, then it is probably because you were dating a senior. Parents have natural worries when their child is dating someone not their age. Be understanding, and look at it from their perspective. Parents tend to be especially anxious when you are dating someone older.

IF YOU'RE THE OLDER ONE

When you are dating someone younger than you, you'll face some good things and some bad things. You may feel less pressure if you are older because people tend to think that older people are wiser—even though this isn't always the case. The younger person in the relationship will probably look up to you and be flattered that an older person is interested. On the downside, there are also some negatives. For example, a difference in age may come along with a difference in maturity level: In high school, a few years can definitely mean a huge difference where this is concerned. Another drawback is that your friends are probably not the same, and it is easier to date someone who has some of the same friends as you.

> *I really liked this one girl, and we dated a few times. Not only was she younger than me, but she didn't hang out with any of the people that I like to be around.*

> *After a while it just got really boring hanging out with her friends, and it didn't work out.*
>
> —Craig, Heritage High School, Littleton, Colorado

IF YOU'RE THE YOUNGER ONE

When we switch the scenario and you are the younger person, your parents will really keep a close eye on you—and sometimes rightfully so. As exciting as it is to be so cool that the older kids are interested, you should be careful. Dating an older person is not necessarily wrong, but you've got to be more aware. In high school, kids can grow and change so much in just a few years. If you feel comfortable around older kids, then that's a step in the right direction, but don't let the person you are dating affect the rate at which you grow up. Your parents might give you some good advice on this subject as well, and chances are that if you are open with them, they will feel more comfortable allowing you to date an older person.

If you are mature enough and enjoy spending time with older kids, then dating an older person can be a lot of fun. Also, sometimes dating an older person can give you a chance to get a break from your group of friends and meet some new people. On the other hand, this new group of friends can cause problems, especially because it will probably be more difficult to fit in with older students. Don't abandon all your friends because of your new boyfriend or girlfriend, however: These friendships will be valuable to you long after your boyfriend or girlfriend has left school.

LONG-DISTANCE AND OUT-OF-SCHOOL RELATIONSHIPS

When in high school, many kids try to make a long-distance relationship work. Generally speaking, it's hard to have a relationship with someone you don't see on a regular basis. High school is such a busy time, and this makes it hard to find spare minutes to maintain a relationship across the miles. Long-distance relationships are not impossible, but they are much more difficult to maintain.

> *One of my best friends has been in a long-distance relationship for the past six months, and it has worked well for him. They talk on the phone often and see each other once every month or two. I think both he and his girlfriend enjoy having a relationship that is not incredibly serious or time demanding.*
>
> —PETER, HERITAGE HIGH SCHOOL, LITTLETON, COLORADO

THE DIFFERENT SCHOOLS DILEMMA

In real life, long-distance relationships may mean two people in different states or countries. In high school, it can mean two people at different schools. If two people go to different high schools, it will also take some extra effort to keep the relationship steady.

When you're dating someone from your own school, seeing each other everyday will not only remind you of your boyfriend or girlfriend's existence, but it also will provide some time for you to spend together. If you aren't at the same school, you can spend time together only on weekends. Another reason this type of relationship is difficult is because it may be harder to remain faithful to your girlfriend or boyfriend, especially if girls or boys from your school are showing interest.

Despite all the negatives about dating someone who goes to a different school, such relationships can also work out. One good aspect is that when you don't go to the same school as your girlfriend or boyfriend, the relationship can be a lot less stressful. You won't have to think about your girlfriend or boyfriend every second of every class, and you can treasure the time you do get to spend together. Sometimes dating someone at your school can make you forget that you have other friends. But if your boyfriend or girlfriend goes to a different school, you can spend more time with your friends and concentrate on your schoolwork during the week.

Boyfriends and Best Friends: Striking a Balance

GIRLS' NIGHT OUT OR THAT HOT DATE?

If you or your friend has a boyfriend or girlfriend, you will have to deal with choosing between friends and dates. Putting your friendships on hold is tempting while you go for that hot senior, but when that senior goes for your friend, you still will want to spend time with your friend. You've got to remember that no matter how hot that person seems right now, high school relationships are almost always short-term. Don't lose your friendships altogether for a few months with the local heart throb. No matter how close you and your new beau are, remember your other friends, too. They were the ones who supported you when you were getting enough courage to ask him or her out, and they will be the ones you fall back on when you realize that you aren't meant for each other after all.

Talk with your friends. Usually if your friend is close enough to you, he or she will tell you exactly how he or she feels. If your friend says that he or she would like more of your time and attention, then you should make an effort to oblige. You can have a boyfriend or girlfriend and a group of close friends, too. Communicate and try to make it work.

WHAT IF YOU AND YOUR BEST FRIEND LIKE THE SAME PERSON?

Boyfriends and girlfriends can ruin friendships in other ways as well. If you and your friend both like Jimmy, but Jimmy only likes you, you've got some major decision making to do. Try putting yourself in your friend's shoes; how would you feel if he had gone for your friend instead of you? Before you lose a real friendship for a lame reason, put the whole situation in perspective and do everything you can to preserve the real friendship. At the same time, don't let your friends ruin your social life. If you talk about it up front, you can probably go on the date and keep the friendship.

PARENTAL ENCOUNTERS OF THE THIRD KIND

One of the most anxiety-filled experiences of high school is meeting the parents of your girlfriend or boyfriend. To get over the anxiety, you might as well admit to yourself right now that there is a good chance they won't like you—and that's okay. You won't like your kid's boyfriend and girlfriend either when you get older. It is absolutely amazing how our parents are utterly convinced that there is no one on earth good enough for us.

Anyway, once you get over that very likely possibility, you have nothing to lose. If the parents don't like you, hey, they're normal. If they do like you, you have reason to celebrate. Nevertheless, here are a few tips for making the best possible impression.

1. Remember poise, poise, poise. Make an effort to do the simple things, such as offering a handshake (and making it a firm one) and looking your special someone's parents in the eye.

2. Stick to nonvolatile conversation topics. Don't turn to your boyfriend while his parents are in the room and ask which of the seven local parties he wants to go to that night. Don't talk about politics, guns, sex, drugs, or alcohol.

3. Highlight your good points. If you are a good student, you might talk about the classes you are in when you're asked about school. If you are a good athlete, talk about sports. If you are a musician, talk about music. Put your best foot forward.

4. Ask a few questions. You might want to find out from your boyfriend or girlfriend if his or her parents have a hobby, a favorite sports team, or a job that you might be able to discuss. People (including parents) love to talk about themselves. Ask questions like, "So, I hear you like collecting ant farms. My Aunt Edna collects them, too—when did you start?" Or, "John tells

me that you were the world knitting champion in 1978; have you knitted anything lately?" Okay, maybe you shouldn't ask those exact questions, but you get the idea.

5. Be responsible. Don't bring your boyfriend or girlfriend home after curfew. Remember that if he or she leaves with you, the parents will associate you with whatever happens that evening.

How to Get Out of a Bad Date

If you are on a bad date, you will definitely know it. A date can turn into a bad date for many different reasons, but the main red light is when you don't feel comfortable. Now, we're not talking uncomfortable as in, you can't think of anything to say. I'm talking about those situations when you think to yourself, "My dad would kill my date if he was here now." Dating in high school is all about having fun, and if you aren't feeling comfortable, then chances are you're not having fun. If you're ever out to dinner or a movie and you start to feel like you want to get out, don't ignore your instincts. Get out!

One of the easiest ways is to tell the person that you have to check in with your parents; when you call your parents, you can always ask them to pick you up. Parents will understand. You can also call a big brother or big sister or a friend. When you come back to your date, you can just tell them that you have to go home or that you have a family emergency. Be firm. If you are uncomfortable, don't let your date talk you out of ending the evening.

The reason you are dating is to get to know the other person. If that person is not fun to be around and you don't feel comfortable around him or her, then that date is probably not worth your time and energy.

SAFETY SHOULD BE YOUR FIRST CONCERN

If you feel unsafe for any reason and want to end a date, end it. You don't need a good reason to end a date. If your date starts becoming more aggressive than you would like, be firm. Don't be polite or wait for the situation to get worse. Don't be afraid to say no.

HAVE FUN!

High school relationships are all about having fun. You are meeting different kinds of people and learning which ones you like to spend time with—and which ones you don't. Remember that dating doesn't have to be serious. Dating is such a minor aspect of high school compared to all the other concerns in a your life; don't let it dominate your time. After high school, dating can become more serious, stressful, and time-consuming, so enjoy these years of fun while you aren't bothered by talks about commitment. If you and your sweetheart find yourselves discussing baby names and curtain colors, then you might want to think about whether you are in too deep.

Take advantage of your opportunities. High school flies by faster than you can imagine. Dating in high school can provide a lot of special and fun times, but dating isn't the be all and end all. Keep it in perspective and have fun.

CHAPTER 17

Prom, Homecoming, and Other Dances

It was my junior year, and I kept waiting for someone to ask me to prom. I waited up through a month before, a week before, a day before . . . and I finally gave up. I had even gotten a dress, thinking that my boyfriend would go with me. Well, a month and a half before prom, he dumped me. Needless to say, he was more interested in what Tiffany's prom dress was going to look like. Mine was still hanging in the back of the closet, covered in plastic. On prom night, I was getting ready to watch some old movie with my younger sister when the phone rang. It was a guy I hardly knew, and he asked me if I wanted to go to prom. I was ready to refuse, but then I thought, "Hey, I might as well! What else am I going to do?" I also was somewhat anxious to prove to my ex that I could get a date. So I said yes and ran around trying to do everything that other girls had spent all day on. An hour later, he picked me up, and the whole night was spontaneous and a ton of fun. It wasn't exactly what I'd had in mind, but it was pretty cool.

—JENNIFER, HERITAGE HIGH SCHOOL, LITTLETON, COLORADO

Prom: the day when everyone spends an extra hour (or two or three or four!) in front of the mirror. The night when you spend all that money you've carefully hoarded to buy the perfect dress, the perfect dinner, the perfect date. Your prom night is one of the evenings that you will remember for the rest of your life, so if you wake up the next morning thinking, "Umm, what was all the hype about?" then you probably skipped one of the tips provided in this chapter.

DON'T STRESS OUT!

When you strut onto that dance floor, the last thing you should be thinking is, "God, I'm such a loser! I can't dance! I look disgusting in this, I'm sure of it. Oh no, I bet I have bad breath from that Indian food! Dear God, I can't face my date! I never should have come!" Prom should be fun, not stressful. If you feel self-conscious, you probably look it, so relax, and have fun.

> *When I went to my first prom, I had so many worries. I tried desperately to relax, but there was always that part that kept telling me, "What if you get food stuck in your teeth? What if you trip on the dance floor? What if you make a total fool of yourself in front of your date? What if?. . . What if?. . ."*
>
> *I spent so much time stressing out during the prom that I was miserable the entire time. All I wanted to do was get it over with and go home. Since then I have gotten wiser, and now I don't stress about it. I just have fun and enjoy myself. It really ends up being a more fun and memorable experience that way.*
>
> —CASEY, MILILANI HIGH SCHOOL, MILILANI, HAWAII

Plan Ahead

If you can help it, don't leave prom preparations until the last minute. Some stuff you'll want to look into about a month before, such as how much dinner is going to cost, where you are going afterward, how you are going to get a date, and which lucky person is going to be your date. If you have everything planned by the week before, then you will minimize stress and also get first dibs on stuff such as restaurants, corsages/boutonnieres, rides in your friend's car, and of course, the person you plan to be promming with that evening.

Trust me, you won't want to be rushing around the night of prom trying to find a Great Clips that styles hair or a tuxedo rental store that has a size somewhat close to your own. You know when prom will be, so as soon as you know you're going, get cracking on that stuff.

Getting to the Prom

Okay, so you don't want to pick your date up in your '82 Buick, hoping that the hubcaps don't fall off on the way. But don't let transportation be a cause of stress. If you and your date don't really want to fork out a whole bunch of money for a private car or a limousine, remember that you're probably not the only ones in this situation. Maybe you can go in with some other couples or find a friend who's driving and doesn't mind you coming, too. This can actually work for the best: Another couple can fill those awkward silences that are inevitable if you're with someone you don't know that well.

How Much Will Prom Cost You?

The cost of attending prom can vary greatly, from $100 on up, depending upon what you wear, where you go, and how you get there. However, you do not need to be that big $1,000-plus spender to have a good time. The cost of prom is usually marked by the cost of your ticket, evening gown/tuxedo, boutonniere/corsage, photographs, limousine (optional), nails/makeup appointments, and after-prom activity.

TICKETS

The cost of prom tickets differs from school to school but is usually determined by the area at which the event is held. If your prom is held in the school gymnasium, the cost will be lower than if it is held in a banquet hall or hotel. Proms held on the school campus are usually about $20 to $30 per couple. Proms held in banquet halls and hotel ballrooms that provide dinner take a bigger price jump to about $80 to $140 per couple.

A tip for the gals: If your prom bid range is in the $80 to $140 range, suggest splitting the cost between the two of you. Usually, guys have trouble suggesting that kind of stuff, and end up getting stressed out about all the money. If he does insist on paying, it's perfectly okay to let him do so.

ATTIRE

With clothing trends coming and going, it's hard to say what exactly is "in" and "out." Formal-wear shops have catalogs that can help you make your clothing decision.

> *I personally am not one to wear something just because it is "in"; I wear what appeals to me. Whether it falls into the "in" or the "out" category has little or no weight in my decision.*
>
> —CASEY, MILILANI HIGH SCHOOL, MILILANI, HAWAII

For the Guys

The cost for renting a tuxedo is usually about $50 to $120, depending on the brand and accessories. Shoes may also be included in the tuxedo package. If you are planning to buy your tux, the price is pretty high, depending on the brand. A new tux can cost from $200 to $1,000, which is usually too much to spend for one night.

Guys, though you are the lucky ones because you don't need to make all of those "beauty" appointments for prom, you have a host of other concerns to occupy your time:

- Make sure you get your tuxedo early enough: Average sizes are sometimes all out if you don't get to the shop early.

- Don't forget to find out what your date will be wearing so that you can plan your tux and the corsage you will probably want to buy. Basically, you don't need to spend too much time getting ready. But, guys, don't totally downplay the situation. I mean, you will want to spend some time primping. After all, this is prom!

> *I had borrowed my tuxedo pants, and I didn't try them on until about an hour before I had to meet at my date's house for pictures. Well, they were way too big, and I had to tape them up because I borrowed them and didn't want to hem them. The tape didn't stick at all to the material, and it kept falling down all night. When I got to my date's house, her dad pulled me aside and showed me where it had fallen out and that the tape was dragging. All night I had to keep going into the bathroom and checking that it hadn't fallen down with all these pieces of tape hanging from the bottom.*
>
> —PETER, HERITAGE HIGH SCHOOL, LITTLETON, COLORADO

For the Girls

Girls usually don't rent a prom dress. Many girls shop around with their friends or parents to purchase a prom gown for that special night. Just about every clothing store sells evening gowns, which means that the hardest part will not be finding a place that sells dresses, but picking a dress from the wide selection. The price range for a prom dress is usually around $75 to $300.

Whether or not buying a dress is on your agenda, you'll have a few things you need to take care of before you're ready for prom night:

- If you are looking for a new dress, go shopping at least two weeks before the big night, in case the store has to order your size or the color you want, or in case every single dress you find seems to look hideous on you.

- If spending a bundle on a new dress is freaking you out, you can always ask your sister or friends for their old (which translates to "used once") prom dress.

- If you're planning to get your hair, nails, or makeup done, then keep in mind that school proms usually occur around the same time, so salons tend to get booked up early. Also, when you arrive, you might want to let the salon know what your dress looks like. Certain styles look better with certain dresses.

- Tell your date what color dress you will be wearing so that he can plan his tuxedo and corsage.

One time, I bought my dress two months before prom, and when prom night came around, it was way too big! It looked awful—I guess I had lost a lot of weight—but I had to pin it in all these different places, and I kept worrying about my date getting poked! Now I always try on everything a week before, just in case.

—JACQUELYN, MILILANI HIGH SCHOOL, MILILANI, HAWAII

To me, gown shopping with my friends is one of the joys of prom. It's a chance for me to spend time with just the girls and spend my parents' money!

—JILL, KAILUA HIGH, KAILUA, HAWAII

CORSAGES

The custom is that the guy purchases a corsage or buys flowers (preferably roses) for his date. There are two main types of corsages: 1) a pin-on corsage; and 2) a wear-around-her-wrist corsage. An alternative to the corsage is roses. Roses come in various colors, each with its own special meaning:

Red signifies love and respect.

Confetti signifies festivity and magnetism.

Peach signifies desire.

Pink signifies joy, grace, and poetic romance.

White signifies innocence and secrecy.

Yellow signifies friendship and joy.

Champagne signifies gaiety, freedom, and pleasure.

Roses can be displayed in various ways, with the most popular the hand-held French bouquet. This type of bouquet is short, neat, and easier to carry than the long-stem rose bouquets. The price for a French bouquet is usually around $20 to $45, depending upon the florist and time of order.

If you decide to buy a corsage, the price range for that is around $15 to $45. You will probably have the choice of a pin-on or a wrist corsage. We recommend opting for the wrist corsage when in doubt: Some dresses don't have a good place to pin on a corsage, and the wrist corsage is also much easier to put on and take off.

Ask your friends what they are doing. You don't want to your date to be carrying around roses if everyone else has a corsage.

BOUTONNIERES

What girls traditionally get for their date is a boutonniere, which is a pin-on carnation or rose accented with baby's breath. The boutonniere is worn on the right lapel of the tuxedo. The price for a boutonniere is around $5 to $10.

A boutonniere order for your date should be made about two weeks in advance, and preferably after you have found out what color tuxedo he will be wearing.

Putting on a Boutonniere

Girls, you might want to practice this at home—or ask your mother if she knows how to pin on a boutonniere—because chances are, your date won't have a clue.

1. Hold the boutonniere in place on the lapel, and hold the pin on a diagonal going from top left to bottom right.

2. Push the pin through the thick part of the boutonniere.

3. Put the pin into the lapel, making sure that your hand is behind it to prevent the pin from poking your date.

4. When you bring the pin back up through the lapel, the end of it should go through the curly queue at the end of the bouton- niere, holding the flower in place and upright.

PHOTOGRAPHS

At your prom, photographers will be ready to take posed-couple and group shots. Photos are usually done on a walk-in basis during the prom. Some schools, however, give out numbers and call groups and couples in one by one so that you don't have to waste precious prom time in a line all night.

Pictures usually must be paid for at the prom and run a pretty penny: You may spend about $20 to $75 on prom pictures. The form of payment for these pictures is usually cash, but some companies accept checks with an ID. If you know that Aunt Harriet and Uncle Irving, and all those other relatives you've only met a few times, are going to want prom pictures—and if you want to have enough to give to your friends (and that one extra to send to your ex)—you should order a decent-sized package to fill the demand. Or, you can just skip sending out pictures to your relatives; you might not want to have a picture with some date you barely know on your relative's refrigerator for years to come.

It might be a good idea to bring a disposable camera (about $12 at the local grocery store) with you to the prom. You'll have fun going wild with the pictures, and it's likely that those pictures will be the most memorable of all.

As for the decision on who pays for the professional pictures, splitting the cost is probably the best road.

What Can We Do to Make Prom More Fun?

Everyone wants to make the most out of their prom, but few like to make plans on what to do and usually end up driving around all night doing nothing. Doing so will kill the fun; nobody likes driving around doing nothing unless there are sights to see.

Now when we say "make a plan," we don't necessarily mean get a paper and pencil and write down the definite evening plans—we just mean that you should think about it and have options on what to do for the night.

1. Go in groups.

Prom is always more enjoyable with your friends. Couples can share a car or meet up somewhere and arrive at the dance at the same time. Talk to your friends beforehand about getting a group together.

> *Before our school prom, my date and I met up with a bunch of our friends at the city mill parking lot. We sat there and chatted for a while, laughing and taking pictures of each other. At the prom we all danced together and had the time of our lives; afterward we rented a hotel room and stayed up all night*

> *pillow fighting and telling stories to each other. That night is a night that I will remember for the rest of my life. From then on, our group was a lot closer.*
>
> —IAN, MILILANI HIGH SCHOOL, MILILANI, HAWAII

2. PLAN FOR AFTER-DANCE FUN.

It's a bummer to call it a night right after prom, so find something to top off the night. You can do anything from playing laser tag to heading to the beach or going on carnival rides.

Some schools have an organized after-prom party, which is usually a relatively cheap activity that's a lot of fun and can be a great way to round out the evening with a bunch of friends.

> *I personally look forward to the after-prom activity more than the actual prom itself. After the prom, I can get out of my stiff formal wear and get a little looser. Usually around this time I am down to my last penny, as are all of my friends, so we like to cruise the strip of Waikiki and see the free sights and sounds that make Hawaii special.*
>
> —CASEY, MILILANI HIGH SCHOOL, MILILANI, HAWAII

Wherever you live, you can still have a great time. Just remember to stay safe—and, most of all, *have fun!*

PROM HORROR STORIES

Just in case you're still nervous, we thought you might like some fellow students to sympathize with as you are thinking ahead about your prom-to-be.

It was the night before prom, and I was really excited about the next night. I was going with Jason—who, might I add, was the finest guy in the whole school. In order to look as slim as possible in my dress, I skipped dinner that night and only ate a bagel the next morning. An hour before Jason came to pick me up, I had my dress on, and it fit perfectly. I was really hungry, but the pain was bearable. Well, he picked me up, and on the way there the famine really hit me because I was so hungry! Once we got to the restaurant, I headed straight for the food bar. I figured I would eat just enough to hold me off for a while. I started with one chicken wing, then two, then some potato salad, roast beef, Jell-O, and pie—the next thing you know, I was pigging out in front of everyone at my table! I didn't realize that before the prom my dress fit perfectly, and pigging out would alter that state. Well, I finished eating and went to the dance with my date. I made it through the slow dances, but when the fast songs came along my dress ripped from the back! The worst part was that I didn't realize it until my date told me. I was so embarrassed that I left the prom without my date. I haven't heard from him since.

—Crystal, Pearl City High School, Pearl City, Hawaii

After our prom, my date took me to an ice cream shop for dessert. Waiting for me there was a giant chocolate cheesecake and a tub of vanilla ice cream. While I was pigging out on the cheesecake, I leaned over the table to get a bite of ice cream, which my date was eating. While leaning over I fully dipped the front of my white dress into the cake! I ruined my dress and haven't heard the end of it from my date since!

—Kathryn, Mililani High School, Mililani, Hawaii

HOMECOMING AND OTHER SCHOOL DANCES

One of the main differences between middle school and high school in the social department is the number of homecoming and other school dances—and the hype surrounding them—throughout the year. Dress for these occasions is usually casual or based on a particular theme—*casual* meaning what you usually wear, and *theme* meaning dress like a hippie if the theme is '60s night.

> *I prefer school dances to prom because they're a lot cheaper and the stress level is greatly reduced. I can have fun, dance, and do things afterward just as I could for prom without all the "red tape."*
>
> —JESSICA, BILOXI, MISSISSIPPI

Homecoming is a week filled with numerous activities, including a parade, football game, and big dance. Participation in the parade and assemblies is free, so get out, show some spirit, and have fun.

> *To me, homecoming takes time out of classes; although some complain that the assemblies get boring, I just think of math class and it gets a lot more fun.*
>
> —CASEY, MILILANI HIGH SCHOOL, MILILANI, HAWAII

Prom, winter ball, homecoming, and all the other dances in between are all for your enjoyment. Forget about your problems and have fun. If you are wondering whether you should ask someone to go, do it. You'll regret it that night if all your friends are out having a good time and you're watching TV reruns.

CHAPTER 18

Alcohol and Drugs

One of the main decisions you will have to make in high school involves the issue of drugs and alcohol. No matter what type or size of high school you attend, there will be undoubtedly opportunities to drink or do drugs. This is a really important decision, and one that you should make for yourself before you're put on the spot at that party. Trust me: There have been too many who learned this the hard way and who went along with their friends, did something they didn't really want to do, and paid the consequences.

—MERRITT, HERITAGE HIGH SCHOOL, LITTLETON, COLORADO

Entering high school brings many new challenges. One of the most difficult to deal with is the issue of alcohol and drugs. Chances are that if you are a teenager in America today, you will confront situations involving either alcohol or drugs. *High School Survival*, of course, does not endorse underage drinking. However, to handle these inevitable encounters, every teenager ought to think about how he or she will handle situations involving drugs and alcohol.

We all are well aware of what our parents want us to do and what is okay or not okay with them. And we also all know that "just saying no" is a whole lot easier said than done. Thus, many teenagers struggle with peer pressure and situations that are uncomfortable and hard to get out of safely.

Before you can make any sort of decision, you must know what it is that you are saying yes or no to. Following are 10 important facts about teenage drinking.

1. Alcohol is absorbed into the bloodstream.

Alcohol is swallowed, which means that it will be digested and must flow throughout your entire body. Your body starts absorbing it as soon as it enters your mouth. Once the alcohol reaches the stomach, it is slowly absorbed into the bloodstream, which is taken through your whole body and which will eventually affect every part of it as well. Alcohol can also be absorbed through the small intestine as well as the colon, so just because someone throws up (usually from drinking too much), that does not mean that the alcohol will stop being absorbed by the body.

2. The effects of alcohol last a long time.

The effects of alcohol often are felt within 10 minutes of one drink. But sometimes it takes a lot longer for someone to feel this, which often causes people to drink more and can lead to dangerous situations. Even if you drink and you don't get sick from the liquor, it still is dangerous because it will stay in your body for so long. An average adult's liver can process about one drink per hour. But if you are smaller, or if your body just doesn't process alcohol as quickly, it can take much longer. The effects of alcohol can last 1 to 12 hours.

3. Alcohol use has many physical consequences.

Some of the immediate effects of alcohol include blurred speech, lack of muscular coordination (such as stumbling while walking), depression, aggression, dizziness, disorientation, double vision, memory and comprehension loss, shallow respiration, nausea, and decreased inhibitions (which means that your conscience is shot, including the little guy that tells you when you are doing something stupid). Some long-term effects of alcohol also can be emotional, while others often include physical dependence on liquor, brain damage or early death, digestive system disorders (ulcers, pancreatitis, cirrhosis of the liver), blackouts, brain disorders, vitamin deficiencies, and malnutrition.

4. EVERYONE REACTS TO ALCOHOL DIFFERENTLY.

Just because your best friends can drink a lot and have fun does not mean that you will be able to do the same thing. Blood alcohol consumption depends on many different factors and affects everyone differently. One of these factors is the amount consumed in one sitting. The faster you drink, the drunker you will get, and the more prone you are to being dangerously ill. Your size, sex, body build, and metabolism are also factors. In addition, the type and amount of food in your stomach may influence your reaction. Although food or beverages cannot interfere with the effects of alcohol on your body once it has entered the blood stream, fruit sugars or other foods can help shorten the time of the alcohol's effect by speeding up elimination of alcohol from the blood.

5. DRIVING AND DRINKING IS HIGHLY DANGEROUS (AND STUPID).

Drinking and *driving* should never be used in the same sentence, especially by a teenager. If you were to get behind the wheel after drinking, not only would you put yourself in danger, but you also would risk harming everyone else in your car. Worse yet, you could hurt someone else on the road. You run the risk of killing yourself—and some innocent person you don't even know.

Driving involves multiple tasks, many of which can change quickly. If you drink and then drive, your reaction time to anything is slowed, and you may not be able to react in time. Many drunk drivers do not even realize that they are looking at a red light until after they have run through it. Alertness disappears when drinking, so driving is a bad idea.

> *Hey, I had this impression that I was able to drive drunk. It was 11:50 p.m., and I had 10 minutes to get home. I knew that I was not able to drive because I had had too much to drink, but at the same time I did not want to miss curfew and have to deal with my mom. So I drove home. I watched the road in a drunken haze as the snow sifted across the street, and when I pulled up to the garage, I realized that I did not even remember*

> *the drive home. I walked into the house and went into my mom's bedroom to check in with her and tell her I was home. She smelled the liquor on me and immediately knew I had been drinking. I got grounded for the next few weeks, and as I look back on that drive home, I am one of the luckiest kids alive. I am lucky I did not kill myself or someone else.*
>
> —BOB, DENVER, COLORADO

6. DRINKING AND DRIVING IS ILLEGAL.

As a minor, if you have even put a drop of liquor in your mouth and you get behind the wheel, you are breaking the law. If your friends are telling you that they got away with it, remember that *you* may not. If you get pulled over, you risk getting tickets for Minor in Possession, DWAI (Driving While Ability Impaired), DUI (Driving Under the Influence), or whatever other creative infractions your state or a judge might use to punish underage drinkers. Drinking under 21 years of age is illegal by itself, but drinking and driving is stupid, and the punishment may be severe. Losing your license for several years may be the least of your problems.

7. YOU CAN HELP SOMEONE WHO IS IN DANGER FROM DRINKING TOO MUCH.

If someone has been drinking too much and you can help, you should know what to do. Here are a few tips:

- If he or she is throwing up, give your friend water, fresh air, and plenty of room to breathe.

- If your friend has passed out, you might carry him or her to a safer place. Don't lay your friend on his or her back because if your friend begins to vomit while passed out, he or she may choke. Lay your friend on his or her side, and make sure he or she can breathe.

- There's a good chance that a person who has passed out may need medical attention. Find the nearest adult, someone who can help, or someone who you trust. Call your friends' parents.

If you cannot find someone to help, then you should call 911. Better to be safe than sorry.

- Don't be afraid to ask for help. You probably will not get into trouble, and you may be avoiding much larger problems. Just remember that you are doing someone that may be the biggest favor of your friend's life!

> *One day I was hanging out with my friends when we all decided to drink. I decided it would be fun to drink with them, you know, to have a good time. I took a few shots of vodka and decided that it was not enough. So I had a few more—and then a few more. Soon I was so drunk that I could not even speak English. I do not even remember any of this story, but I am writing it based on what my friends have told me. I kept passing out and I could not stand up on my own. I threw up all over my best friend's car (thank goodness I have great friends who were there to help me), and eventually my friends worried enough about my health that they took me home to my parents. It was bad enough that I had let my parents down by drinking, but on top of that I had scared many people I care about half to death and had embarrassed my parents tremendously because they had guests over. I wish I had understood how dangerous drinking was so I would have made a smarter decision.*
>
> —EMILY, GEORGE WASHINGTON HIGH SCHOOL, DENVER, COLORADO

8. DON'T LET PEER PRESSURE DICTATE WHAT YOU'RE DOING.

Peer pressure is probably one of the hardest issues a teenager faces. Remember that *you* are the only one who can decide what you are going to do. Your friends can tell you whether they want you to do it or not, but only you can decide if you will. If you are around kids who are pressuring you to do stuff that you do not feel comfortable doing, you should be questioning how good of friends they are. But at the same time, the truth is that some very good and cool friends may be telling you to do stupid things. So, instead of telling you that you need to drop them and find a new group, we think the better solution may be to think about how you will deal with a peer-pressure situation ahead of time. Below are a few tips to help you resist peer pressure in situations when you want to make your own decisions.

BEFORE YOU CONFRONT PEER PRESSURE

- Decide what you think about drinking before you confront it. Chances are that if you have never thought about it before you try it, you will cave under the peer pressure because that is the easiest choice. But if you have decided beforehand that you do not want to drink, you will be a lot more likely to resist it when the choice is before you.

- Be firm in your choices. If you voice your decision even before you are in a specific situation with alcohol or drugs, you will have a lot less difficulty resisting the pressure because your friends will not be as likely to bug you about it. If your friends know where you stand, they may not even ask you—plus, they'll likely respect you for it.

- Believe in your decision. This is perhaps the most important tip. If you believe in your decision, you will be more likely to be firm about it when the occasion arises to try drinking. Your peers will put less pressure on you because peer pressure tends to increase when people detect insecurity; it usually happens when people believe they can influence you.

When I was making friends at my new high school, I remember overhearing a conversation some people were having about a party that was going on over the weekend. They talked about how they were going to decide who was going to be the D.D. (Designated

> *Driver). I spoke up and told them that I would be happy to be the D.D. because I was not interested in drinking and I would rather be the one with the control over the situation. I remember that my offer was welcomed, but once I got to the party, my friends still asked me if I wanted to have a drink. I firmly said no and they all sort of snorted and then left me alone. I continued to enjoy myself at the party for the most part, realizing that deep down most of my friends were probably happy with my decision because I was holding their lives in my hands by driving them around. My friends have a lot of respect for my decisions and that I hold firm to them, and many of them have given up pressuring me to do stuff I don't want to.*
>
> —Katie, East High School, Denver, Colorado

When You Are in the Situation

We all get there. No matter how hard we try to avoid it, and no matter how much our parents shelter us from it, we all get to be around alcohol or drugs at some point. And sometimes it is nice to know exactly how to handle those hard situations.

- When you go out with your friends, make sure that you have a driver you can trust, especially once you and your friends start to drive. Choose someone who won't let you down by drinking.

- Tell your friends if you feel uncomfortable. Chances are that your friends will be as uncomfortable as you are, if not more so.

- Call someone if you are in trouble. As afraid as you might be to call a parent or a trusted family friend, realize that those closest to you will be happy you showed good judgment: They care about your safety.

- Be responsible and firm. Get out of any uncomfortable situation as fast as you can. If you do not feel good about a situation, you probably should not be there.

DRUGS

The same tips that apply to alcohol also apply to drugs. Drugs are potentially more serious because their direct effects and side effects are potentially more mind altering and more lethal. Use good judgment.

The most common drug you will probably come across in high school is marijuana. Marijuana is often referred to as *weed, pot, bud, hash, dope, grass,* and *kind.* Marijuana is smoked for its intoxicating effects. The primary ingredient that produces the mind-altering reactions is delta-9-tetrahydrocannabinol (THC). The level of THC determines the potency of the drug and can range from 0.01 to 10 percent (10 percent is 1,000 times more potent that 0.01 percent). Although marijuana is not believed to be physically addictive, it can be mentally addicting because people begin to rely on its effects. Heavy usage of marijuana can lead to a loss of motivation and indifference toward goals and future plans.

Ultimately, you have to make your own decisions about alcohol and drugs. Use good judgment. Don't be afraid to get yourself out of uncomfortable situations. Make sure that you are in control. High school can be a lot of fun, so don't ruin the whole experience by making one bad decision that forces you to grow up faster than you ever wanted.

CHAPTER 19

Cars

I was so excited to drive, and I heard all my friends' stories about the new cars they were getting. My parents laughed at my attempts to ask for my own car, so my 16th birthday came and I was looking forward to riding the bus with a license in my pocket. Then I had a dream come to life. I was totally surprised when one of my birthday presents was a used purple pick-up truck. It wasn't exactly a beauty, but to me it looked perfect.

—PETER, HERITAGE HIGH SCHOOL, LITTLETON, COLORADO

Getting a car means major changes in a teenager's life. Suddenly you can drive to school and pick up your friends—and, best of all, you don't have your parents waiting to drive you home after everything you do. All high school students dream of driving a car, so you probably don't need advice on how to enjoy your newfound freedom.

Unfortunately, there's a lot of responsibility that goes along with those cool machines. We teenagers have a bit of a reputation surrounding our driving abilities. To our parents, there are few scarier things in today's world than to let a teen loose with a car. Most problems, however, can be avoided using simple responsibility and common sense.

YOU THOUGHT HISTORY CLASS WAS BORING?

Before you ever get to drive on your own, you will probably have to go through the torture formally called driver's ed. Yes, the local stamp-collecting convention would be more fun. Never fear, though: We have compiled a few tips to help you through both the hours in the classroom and the hours on the road that will best prepare you for when you start driving:

1. TAKE THE CLASS EARLY.

We all have better things to do than spending a week or more of our free time in a classroom, but it will pay off to get an early start. If you can, take driver's education in the summer (or whenever you have the most time to spare). Most importantly, though, make sure to take the class early enough to get your license as soon as you turn 16. Don't be the procrastinator who has to wait to get his license (how frustrating!).

2. FIGHT THROUGH THE BOREDOM AND PAY ATTENTION.

In driver's ed, you learn important stuff about driving in different conditions, the state driving laws, and everything else you'll need to be a good driver. If you've never been behind the wheel, these things may not seem important, but you will soon be wishing you had paid more attention. Besides, all that stuff shows up on the written portion of the test you have to take to get the Holy Grail for teenagers: your license.

3. USE YOUR PERMIT.

At some point before you turn 16 (hopefully), you will get a permit allowing you to drive with adults. From that point until you get your license, you should be *driving with adults!* The more driving practice you have before you get your license, the better driver you will be; there's no reason not to utilize that time. Most driver's ed companies do on-the-street driving with an instructor. Driving with a stranger in the passenger seat watching your every move is very stressful, but it will help you. Also, make sure that you are driving as much as possible when your parents are in the car with you during your permit phase (tell them you need the practice!).

> *I used to hate having to drive with my dad and would plead with him to take the wheel (of course, he never did), but when I turned 16 I felt more comfortable driving than most of my friends.*
>
> —Mike, George Washington High School, Denver, Colorado

Putting It to the Test

After your months of training, you will come to your driver's test. If you have been practicing, you'll do fine, but there are ways to make it go smoother.

1. *Relax!* The more nervous you are behind the wheel, the worse you will do. If you just have confidence in your driving ability and concentrate on the road, you won't have any problems. Remember, though, that if you do fail, it's not the end of the world. You can retake the test as many times as you need until you pass.

2. *Practice, practice, practice!* You have to be very comfortable driving before you get behind the wheel for your test.

> *The first time I took the driver's test was awful. First, I had to parallel park and was so nervous that I couldn't do it. Then we slowly began to exit the parking lot, and I immediately stalled. Then we came upon an intersection where I was supposed to turn right. I pulled up to the intersection as the light turned yellow. Without hesitation, I took the right turn. Imagine my surprise when the instructor promptly informed me that I had just failed my driving exam. I would not have been so nervous or made so many mistakes if I just would have practiced driving enough to become comfortable before the test.*
>
> —Katie, George Washington High School, Denver, Colorado

3. *Drive like a veteran.* The instructor does not want to see how you handle tight turns while going 30 mph, or how you weave in and out of traffic. Make the test as easy as possible by going slow (but not too slow) and making sure every move is a legal one. Smooth starts and stops (and no stalls) are important.

GETTING WHEELS AND KEEPING THEM

Once you pass your test, turn 16, and get your license, you may or may not get the use of a car. The issue of whether you get to drive a car is something that each teen has to work out with his or her parents. Quite a few factors play into this decision, such as money, safety, and responsibility issues. Remember that the goal of your parents is not to keep you locked up at home; most of the time they are looking out for your well-being (or the well-being of everyone else on the road!).

If your parents decide to allow you to drive, you are set free on the road of life. Many accidents and tickets happen within the first year (and even the very first day!) of getting a license, so it is important to try your best to start out as a good driver. Here are some tips to help you.

1. BEFORE YOU START DRIVING, KNOW HOW YOUR SPECIFIC CAR WORKS.

Knowing how your car works means understanding how to turn on headlights, defrosters, turn signals, windshield wipers, and so on. You don't want to be fumbling with those controls on the road. This also means knowing any of the unique quirks that give your car its personality. Do you have to push the emergency brake down three clicks to make it work? Is it remarkably difficult to find third gear? Do your blinkers turn on when you change the radio station? (Okay, if the latter happens, you probably shouldn't be driving that car. . . .)

2. DON'T SPEED!

Driving too fast leads to tickets and accidents, especially if you are just beginning to drive. It feels great to hit that accelerator and zoom away, but it's really dangerous. You might think you have control of the car, but when the person in front of you comes to a dead stop, you're out of luck. Some people, of course, speed to get where they're going more quickly. In the end, it really doesn't make much of a difference, maybe one or two minutes at the most on a half-hour drive. Your best bet for showing up on time is leaving on time. Cops love to prey on teenagers; it's just not worth the risk.

3. FOR THOSE WHO CAN'T FOLLOW THE LAST TIP, CHECK OUT THIS ONE.

If you do have a lead foot, know when you absolutely have to slow down. Obviously, if you see a police car, hit the brakes. If you drive some of the same streets on a daily basis, you will begin to notice some speed traps. Be careful and be smart. Driving tickets send your insurance premiums to the stratosphere. Finally, don't ever speed around a lot of traffic. You end up weaving in and out of traffic and are a lot more likely to cause an accident. While a ticket may be a problem, your primary concern should be safety. Remember that a ticket is only money, while an accident could cost you your life—or perhaps someone else's.

4. PAY ATTENTION.

Don't space out while you're driving. It's so easy to start playing with the radio, or talking with your friend in the passenger seat, or just start thinking about your day at school, that math test you have to study for, or that cute freshman in your English class. Before you know it, your car is mangled, and you just lost driving privileges for the next 30 years. When you drive, keep your eyes and thoughts completely on the road.

5. BE EXTRA CAREFUL WHEN YOU ARE DRIVING FRIENDS AROUND.

The easiest time to loose your focus is when you get into a conversation with the passengers. You don't have to be a mute, but keep conversation to a minimum.

6. MUSIC IN THE CAR SHOULD BE NO LOUDER THAN THE AVERAGE POLICE SIREN.

If you blast that favorite CD of yours on the road, you might not hear the horn of that person you are about to sideswipe. Music also can distract you from paying attention to the road. Despite these dangers, you will learn that your car stereo will become your closest companion while you're driving. By no means should you not listen to any music (after all, that's half of what makes driving fun), but keep it low, and resist the temptation to reach over and change the channel after every song.

7. WATCH OUT FOR BAD WEATHER.

In rain, snow, or icy conditions, drivers (including you) tend to lose control of their cars. This means that accidents in these conditions are pretty frequent. If you think to yourself "Hey, I live in Tennessee—it only snows once in a blue moon, so I can forget this one," think again! Driving carefully in bad conditions is even more important when none of the other people on the road have a clue about driving in a foot of snow.

Four-wheel drive helps a little, but by no means does it make a car invincible to the effects of snow. In fact, four-wheel drive only helps you accelerate, and most accidents happen when people are trying to stop.

Even if it's not a ton of fun, though, there's no need to hibernate every time it snows. Don't freak out if you do need to drive in bad conditions; just drive defensively and be even more aware of your surroundings. The basic rules of thumb are to never make sharp movements and, if you spin out, to steer in the direction of the spin. Tough conditions require such different driving styles, so if you think you might be in situations with snow or ice, make sure to practice at least a little on snow or ice—preferably with an experienced driver in the car—before you get your license.

8. WATCH OUT WHEN YOU ARE BACKING UP.

Many accidents in the first year of driving happen when you are backing up and forget to look behind you. Crash! You just hit your neighbor's car across the street. Make sure to do more than check the mirrors when you back up your car. Turn your head around and actually look. Sometimes you'll be surprised to find out there's a parked car behind you.

9. DON'T DRINK AND DRIVE.

Duh. You've heard it 2,000 times in your life, and should probably hear it 20,000 times more. It may happen that you will drink when you weren't planning on it, and you'll have to be home at a certain time that night. Just remember that your parents would rather get a call from you saying you had a drink or two and don't want to drive and are just going to stay at a friend's house than to get a call the next morning from the police reporting an accident. Even if you don't get in an accident, a DUI ticket is severe enough to take away your license, put you into quite a lot of debt and trouble, and give you a police record. If you must be somewhere, call a cab or get a ride with a sober friend. It's just not worth the risk to drive when you're drunk.

A year ago, I was at a party with some friends. At the time, I had about three close friends: John, Nick, and Kevin. Kevin was a pretty big guy—I mean, whenever we did the guy thing and wrestled each other, he always won. Anyway, at this party, he got totally wasted. John, Nick, and I told him to get a ride with someone or call a cab, but he was very aggressive and brushed us away and cussed us out. Like the cowards we were, we left the keys in his hand. I got a call the next day from the school. Kevin had sped through a red light and smashed into another car. When the ambulance arrived, they tried to get him out, but his skull was smashed. The car he hit contained a young mom and her baby, who both died that night.

I was so shocked. I thought, "This is something that you read about. This is one of those ads on TV. This can't happen to me. My friend can't be dead." But he was, and even today, I can't tell this story without crying.

> *I saw the father of the baby and mother that he killed. He was playing a tape of his wife teaching their son to talk, just listening to their voices over and over. I can't even describe what it's been like to know that I left him with the keys in his hand. You may think the consequences are bad if your parents find out, but it's not worth it to risk this much. And if you're a true friend, you'll know it's not worth it. Just remember.*
>
> —ANONYMOUS

Also, when you are driving (sober) late at night, you have to look out for other drunk drivers. If any car seems to be swerving at all, changing speeds a lot, or acting strange in any other way, the driver is probably drunk. Do your best to avoid those cars because they could cause an accident at any time. Pull over and give those cars some space, let them get out of sight, and then continue on your way.

On a similar note, never carry alcohol in your car. If parents or cops ever find it, it would be safe to say that you would not be in a good situation. Alcohol and cars should under no circumstances be related.

10. WEAR YOUR SEATBELT.

Wearing your seatbelt goes without saying. Also remember to tell your passengers to put on theirs if you are driving. Your passengers will respect you more as a driver if you remind them to buckle up.

WHEN BIG BLUE CATCHES YOU

For most of us this is "when," not "if"—even if you are a good driver, you may get at least one ticket or have one accident (or both) in high school. The most important thing to remember is that these things happen (that's why you have insurance). Here are a few tips to keep in mind for those sorry occasions.

1. STAY CALM!

When you see those flashing lights in your rear-view mirror, don't freak out. Pull over slowly and try to remain calm.

> *When I was driving for only the third time in my life (at midnight), I was pulled over by a cop. When I first saw those flashing lights in my rear view mirror, my heart jumped into my throat. Fortunately, I had not been speeding, so I knew I wasn't in big trouble. It turns out that the cop just wanted to tell me that one of my headlights was out and that I should get it replaced. I still almost had a heart attack.*
>
> —MIKE, GEORGE WASHINGTON HS, DENVER, COLORADO

2. DON'T ASSUME THE WORST.

Contrary to popular teen culture, cops are not evil monsters whose sole intent it is to make life miserable for high school students. Most policemen are quite reasonable to talk to and understand the situation you are in when they are standing there in front of you. Unless you have a very good reason for doing whatever the cop pulled you over for, don't argue. Arguing usually makes it worse. Crying tends not to work, either. Just be polite and courteous. That usually works best.

> *I was late to pick up my date, who lived about 10 miles away, so I hit the gas and went about 80 MPH. Too worried about being late, I didn't realize how fast I was going. Lucky for me, the blue lights that soon flashed behind me helped remind me. The cop pulled me over and gave me the famous line: "Do you know how fast you were going?" I knew I was already busted, so I answered "No, but I'm sure you do." The cop was amused and asked me where I was heading off to. I*

> *told him I had to pick up a date and was already late.*
> *He sympathized with me and was sure to write up the*
> *ticket just as fast as he could—what a guy huh?*
>
> —Casey, Mililani High School, Mililani, Hawaii

3. Tell the 'rents.

As tough as it is to tell parents about a ticket, they need to know. It might show up on insurance anyway, or maybe they can help you fight the ticket in court if you feel the need to do so. Your parents will find out eventually, and it's usually best coming from you. Remember that they've probably gotten a ticket or two in their life. If you are truly sorry, your parents usually will be somewhat understanding.

What About Accidents?

Accidents can be even scarier, but you should handle them as calmly and productively as you can. Here are a few tips on handling accidents.

1. If your accident is minor (without injury or too much damage), exchange information and phone numbers with the other party and notify the police later. Make sure to get all the necessary info: full name, telephone number, address, insurance company, and license plate number.

2. If the accident is more serious, you probably should call the police on the spot.

3. Never try to decide whose fault the accident is at the scene. Deciding fault only leads to anger and frustration. If there is a question, the police or insurance will look into it. In most cases, your insurance company needs to be notified, which your parents can help you with that day.

> *Three months after I got my license, my parents left town and let me drive the new $20,000 Volvo for the week. One of the very first nights they were gone I was driving with some friends. I pulled up behind a flatbed tow truck at an intersection. The truck turned left, so I proceeded to drive across the intersection. The truck started backing up! I honked the horn but it was too late. The truck smashed the driver's side window and back seat window and shattered the windshield. Even though it was the truck driver's fault, the first thing she said when she got out of the truck was "These stupid teenage drivers, I can't believe you did this. What does a 16-year-old know about driving?" I called my parents, and they were pretty upset. It ended up costing $9,000 to fix and took the rest of the summer. Needless to say, I don't get to drive that car much anymore!*
>
> —MEGAN, GEORGE WASHINGTON HIGH SCHOOL, DENVER, COLORADO

4. The only basic rule regarding accidents is that when someone is rear-ended, the car in back is almost always at fault. If you are on the highway going 60 mph and the car in front of you stops to let a squirrel cross the road, any damage you might do to that car is your fault. So leave plenty of space and watch out for those break lights.

5. Never leave the scene of an accident, even if you're not at fault. Not only is this inconsiderate, but it could land you in quite a bit of trouble. That goes for parked cars and stationary objects as well. It's real easy to take off if you nick a car in a parking lot, but try putting yourself in that driver's shoes when he or she comes back to a damaged car and has no way to pay for the repairs. At least leave your name and a phone number where you can be reached. More often than not, the person will be so appreciative of your good deed that you won't have any consequences at all.

6. Finally, the best way to minimize risk during an accident is to wear your seatbelt and require everybody else in your car to wear one as well. We don't mean to be repetitive, but it's simple, easy, and the best way to keep your head from going through the windshield.

Taking Care of Your Car

Car maintenance also tends to be a problem for teens. This can seem tedious at times, but remember that cars are quite complicated machines and need lots of love and attention to keep them happy and running smoothly. If you treat your car well, it will treat you well. Here's how:

Before you ever start driving, you should know some specific things about your car:

- How to change a flat tire
- How to check your oil
- How to add coolant and washer fluid
- How to jump a dead battery
- The make and model of your car

You never know when a disaster might happen, so it's always good to be ready. If you need to learn how to jump a battery, check your oil, or add washer fluid, ask a parent, a friend, or even an attendant at the local gas station.

OIL, YOUR CAR'S LIFEBLOOD

If you have a pretty old car that's not in great shape, check your oil every time (or every other time) you fill it up with gas. Otherwise, you should check about once a week or so. If you make a habit of checking, you will have a lot easier time remembering to check. You'll hear lots about how oil is the lifeblood of the car, and it's true. If you wait too long to check the oil, you'll be treated to the unfortunate experience of having your engine blow out and knowing that you could have prevented disaster.

Along with checking your oil, you should change it every three months or every 3,000 miles, whichever is shorter. Changing oil yourself is cheaper, but kind of a pain. JiffyLube and other such establishments do a great job with a simple oil change. In addition to your oil, they also will check your other fluids, filter, and so on, all for about $30. It's a pretty good deal.

OTHER CAR CRISES

If you see, hear, or smell any problem with your car, get it checked out immediately. Something small could turn into something big if you aren't careful. Hopefully, your parents generally will have more experience with cars and can help you out—and maybe tell you if you need to take it in to a mechanic.

HAPPY CRUISIN'

Despite all the problems you could face as a high school driver, the fact is that most teen driving experiences are fine. Probably (and especially if you follow the above tips) you will go through high school without a major bad experience behind the wheel. Overall, driving is fun, painless, and a great part of the high school experience. If you are fortunate enough to be driving a car—even if it's not your own—smile and think about some of your friends who are still waiting for their turn behind the wheel.

CHAPTER 20

Fashion and Shopping

I admit I've had it a little easy when it comes to shopping, having a fashion designer for a mother. However, I have had my share of troubles and exasperation on my shopping trips. Through many years of braving the shopping malls with my mom, I've assembled quite an arsenal of tips that help to conquer the crises we all encounter when searching for the perfect outfit.

—Kate, Saint Mary's Hall, San Antonio, Texas

Who says a person can't be academic and fashionable at the same time? Fashion can be one of the most entertaining parts of the high school experience, and a good trip to the mall with friends is a great way to take your mind off the rigors of academic life. Shopping also can be a great way to channel and express your personality and uniqueness. Admittedly, fashion can be a source of stress when you "don't have a thing to wear" to that big party Friday night. However, by following these simple tips, hopefully your experiences with haute couture during your high school years will be much more enjoyable, and you will find yourself always in style!

HOW TO AVOID THE FASHION POLICE (AND HAVE FUN DOING IT)

1. WHAT DO YOU *REALLY* NEED?

One of the most important things to remember as you head out to the mall for your next shopping trip is the difference between what you *need* and what you *want*. It's easy to wander through Abercrombie and Fitch and want to buy everything in the store. But unless you have an unlimited budget for clothes (if you do, please share with the rest of us!), you will need to narrow your selections. To figure out what you will be glad you bought, it's a good idea to go through your wardrobe and find out what essentials you think are missing; that way you can go to stores with an agenda. Shopping at the grocery store, for instance, is much easier if you have already made out a grocery list, and the same standard applies when shopping at the mall. You may love that purple sweater you saw, but having a list will remind you that you have one just like it in blue at home. If you know you just need a pair of jeans and maybe some T-shirts, it's much easier to keep your expenses at a minimum and save your hard-earned bucks for something special.

2. BE WARY OF CLOTHES THAT SEEM TOO TRENDY.

One problem that surfaces easily is the tendency to buy clothes that go out of style quickly. Yes, those 3-inch platform boots would look cute with your new pair of Levi's, but consider the length of time you will really be able to wear them. The problem with ultra-trendy clothes is that they go out of style soon after you buy them. Trends come and go often and unpredictably, and it's expensive to try to keep up with them. That's why it's a good idea to buy classics that will look as good next year as they do now. While a few trendy outfits are always fun, make sure that they aren't over-the-top-fashion that will last only a few weeks before you see your mom's point and decide that the bright orange bell-bottoms are pretty hideous. Your money will go a lot further if you buy only clothes that you will be able to wear at least a couple months, if not years.

3. THE BASIC QUALITY OF YOUR CLOTHES IS VERY IMPORTANT.

Good quality in clothing can make the difference between looking classy and looking wannabe-ish. Pay attention to the material of your clothes and the way they are made. Synthetic fabrics such as acrylics can often look fake, especially if not made well. Also be on the lookout for how the shirt you want to buy is stitched. Sometimes clothing that is less expensive is not made very well. If it looks to you like it might fall apart, chances are that it will. Often, a skirt that is made better will look a lot better than the same skirt made from a cheaper material. This is not to say that you shouldn't buy that cute sweater for $2— there is no law that all clothes must be expensive—but you need to have some basic items that are good quality so that if the cheaper stuff starts falling apart, you at least have something to wear to school. Note that you can often get great deals on very good quality stuff if you look in the right places at the right times. The excuse of "I had nothing to wear" doesn't rest well with the authorities. So make sure that if you are expecting to have a shirt for a long time, it is also planning to be around after the first wear.

4. PERUSE FASHION MAGAZINES AND CATALOGS.

Warning—these can be very tricky. It is very difficult to look through the pages of *Vogue* or *GQ* to find anything practical to wear. However, fashion magazines can be a great source for finding really nice, fashionable clothes. What is important here is that magazines are a great place to get *ideas* for clothing. They give you an idea of what is going on in the fashion world at present by way of hemlines, styles, and trends. This way you can go into the stores in your neighborhood knowing what is stylish at present and then can adapt the clothes you find to those styles.

Catalogs are an even easier link to great styles than fashion magazines because you don't have to deal with the bizarre, unwearable fashions that designers sometimes feature in magazines. Catalogs such as *J. Crew*, while rather expensive, are a great way to get ideas for the kinds of clothes that you want to wear.

5. GET A LITTLE HELP FROM YOUR FRIENDS!

Perhaps the best way of all to get ideas about fashion is from your friends. If you admire the shirt your best friend has on, ask him where he got it. By adapting some of the style ideas from each of your friends and adding your own touches, you can create a style that is perfectly unique and fashionable. An easy way to accomplish this tip is simply by going shopping with your most fashion-conscious friends. Notice the kinds of things they like and the stores where they shop. This will also help you to know how to find the best things in stores and how to pair them stylishly with clothes you already have. Friends can also be an honest source of constructive criticism about what looks best on you.

6. BASICS CAN BE BOUGHT ALMOST ANYWHERE: TRY TO BUY ONLY THOSE SPECIAL OUTFITS AT THE MORE EXPENSIVE STORES.

The key to making the money you spend on clothes go further involves separating basics from more special clothes. For example, white T-shirts can be found at almost any store. The difference is, you can buy one at Banana Republic for $30 and one at Target for $8. Your money will last a lot longer if you go to expensive stores only to buy items that you can't get anywhere else. If you find something really unique and nice at a more upscale store, and if you have enough cash from your last birthday, go ahead and buy it; just don't buy everything you want at that store. Use your discretion about where clothing can be found as you go shopping.

7. VISIT THRIFT AND VINTAGE STORES OFTEN.

First of all, it's important to distinguish between a thrift store and a vintage store. A *vintage store* is a store that sells clothing from a specific era that people would find valuable today, such as from the 1920s or '30s. A *thrift store* is a shop that simply sells any sort of used clothing. Keep in mind that it's difficult to go to a secondhand store of any kind (thrift or vintage) and look for something in particular. If you walk into the Salvation Army knowing that you need a long-sleeve white shirt, you're at the wrong place; chances are, it won't be there. However, that can also be a great aspect of shopping at secondhand stores: You never know what you will find. If you're open to ideas, you may find the perfect outfit, one that you never would have imagined before walking into the store.

Thrift stores such as Goodwill or the Salvation Army are an invaluable source of clothes. The greatest thing about the clothes that you find there is not only that they are usually only a couple of dollars, but they are also one of a kind. When you find a nice shirt at a thrift store, you will hardly ever have to worry about anyone else showing up in the same one. The only drawback to this sort of store is that you have to spend a lot of time sifting through things you don't like to find something that you do. Thrift-store shopping is a much more time-consuming activity than regular shopping.

Vintage stores are also fun places to shop, although they are more expensive than thrift stores. At these types of stores, you can find really unusual clothing. These stores are especially useful if something from another era comes back into style. For instance, in women's fashion today, '40s-style knee-length hemlines are reappearing, so a vintage store would be a great place to find an inexpensive skirt like this.

Just on a random note, vintage and thrift stores are also great places to find blue jeans. You can find great used Levi's at thrift stores.

Check out the super tips below offered by two seasoned thrift-store shoppers.

Have you ever walked into school with that new T-shirt and jeans outfit, only to see 15 other people wearing the exact same outfit? Have you ever gotten sick of people stereotyping you as the "GAP Girl" or the "Abercrombie Fiend"? Do you ever wish you could be different? If so, you should try thrift and secondhand store shopping! Shopping at these stores used to be a little of an embarrassment because it almost meant you were telling the world your income level. Nowadays, however, it's fashionable to be different and go against the crowd by shopping at thrift and secondhand stores.

Personal style does not mean society's style. If the clothes from Contempo Casuals do not fit your personal style, don't wear them. In thrift and secondhand stores, you will find a plethora of clothing to fit any style that personally expresses who you are. Let us take you into the world of thrift and secondhand store shopping. You must always follow these steps:

1. Leave plenty of time in your schedule to shop, and don't plan on running in and out of the store in 10 minutes.

2. Know what you want to buy, but don't picture the color, material, washing instructions, and fit in your mind (you will never find what you really want). Everything is always sorted by type: jeans, T-shirts, size, male, female. But the clothing is rarely sorted by color and never is categorized by brand name.

3. Wear leggings or tight clothes that other clothes can easily fit over; just in case there are no dressing rooms, you want to be able to change quickly in the aisles—and you don't want to have to buy clothes that don't fit.

Thrift stores are usually bustling with activity—and depending on where you shop, there will be a distinct odor to the store. Sometimes it smells like oatmeal, and other times it is a dusty smell. But don't let either of these deter you; they add to your shopping experience!

Thrift and secondhand stores contain large quantities of clothes that will reflect your self-confidence and individuality. Clothes are an outlet of personal expression, and they reflect the person who you are. The most important part of anybody's life is to feel

> *confident, and buying new and often outrageous*
> *clothes will help you to feel more beautiful everyday.*
> *It is easy to succumb to societal pressures, but we*
> *should fight to personalize our lives. We can start with*
> *the simple act of shopping wildly and differently.*
>
> —MORGEN AND ROSIA, JEFFERSON COUNTY OPEN SCHOOL,
> LITTLETON, COLORADO

8. IF YOU LIVE IN A SMALL TOWN, TRAVEL.

Adhering to all these fashion rules is difficult if you live in a tiny town of a few thousand or so, or one that doesn't have a very good fashion market. If you have this problem, set aside a weekend where you can take a trip to a larger city near you.

> *Often I can't find what I'm looking for in my town, so*
> *I take a few hours and drive up to Austin, Texas, a*
> *college town with a much, much better selection than I*
> *can find where I live. Not only does a road trip help*
> *you to find better clothes, but it is also a tremendous*
> *amount of fun that makes for a great weekend!*
>
> —KATE, SAINT MARY'S HALL, SAN ANTONIO TEXAS

9. SIZE ISN'T NEARLY AS IMPORTANT AS FIT.

When you are trying on a pair of pants, it is very easy to want to buy the pair that is two sizes two small for you, simply because of the smaller number on the label. Girls can fall very easily into this trap, but it is imperative that you buy clothes that look good on you, regardless of what the label says. You may be able to fit into shorts that are smaller than you usually wear, but it is much better to have a pair that is the right size because these will look best on you! Don't worry about what size you've bought: No one will see the label and gasp at the size. Just buy the clothes that fit you correctly. Keep in mind also that stores do sometimes mislabel items, so if there aren't any left in your size, check out the other ones—you just might get lucky.

Along these same lines, remember to ask the salesperson if the article of clothing is pre-shrunk. Cotton and materials like it can shrink after you wash them, so it is important to know whether your clothes are going to become too small for you after you wash them once. If it isn't pre-shrunk, try to buy the item a little larger so it will shrink down to the perfect size for you—and stay that way.

10. MAKE SURE YOU ARE COMFORTABLE IN WHATEVER YOU WEAR, BOTH PHYSICALLY AND MENTALLY.

Although this may seem obvious, make sure you are comfortable in the clothes you buy. This tip is most pertinent when it comes to buying shoes. They may feel like they fit pretty well, but get up and walk around in them. Make sure that after wearing them for a while, your feet won't be killing you.

This rule also holds true for the way clothing looks on you and the way you feel when you are wearing it. When you are trying on an outfit, be sure that you are comfortable with the way you look. If you feel silly or uncomfortable in the store, you probably won't be any more comfortable when you try it on at home. Chances are, you shouldn't buy it. Go with your gut instinct about clothes. If they seem too outlandish or make you feel uneasy, try something else.

If you are really unsure about whether to buy something, go ahead and take it home (after checking about the return policy), keeping the tags and the receipt, and try it on again at home. If you put it on and still feel uncomfortable about how you look before you are about to go out, return it.

11. WEAR WHAT LOOKS GOOD ON YOU.

Always wear the clothes that look good on you. If skinny, straight-legged pants are "in" right now but flare jeans look so much better on you, then don't let the fashion mags dictate what you wear. There is more than just one way to look fashionable, so find the style of clothing that works best on your figure and wear that. Use your own judgment when trying on clothes: You are the best judge of how you look in something.

Feeling ridiculous in an outfit, even if it is stylish, is perfectly legitimate. Obviously, everyone's bodies are different, so everyone's style is going to be different. What is fashionable is what you look best in, so sometimes you just have to ditch the designer labels and make your own look.

12. FIND YOUR *OWN* STYLE.

After all these tips, the most important piece of advice of all to being fashionable is finding your very own style. Your style is whatever you want it to be, whether it be laid-back casual, super-model glamorous, or even a mixture of both. Never let anyone tell you something is not "you," because "you" is anything you like! You make your own style, no matter what the fashion gurus at Gucci and Armani extol as "fashionable." The more you let our own personality come through in your clothes, the more stylish and fashionable you will be.

> *My style has one thing to say: "Jennifer wears this!" I like my individual style. Style has the ability to set you apart from others. Style brings your own personal touch to the way you look.*
>
> *I own a lot of stuff that is pretty basic: khakis, black pants, and so on. But even with generic pieces like these, I still maintain a very individual look. The key to my particular style is the unexpected. Unique pieces give my wardrobe a finishing touch. Creative accessories do the trick for me. I like to make my own jewelry and hair ornaments. Put some creativity into your appearance!*
>
> —Jennifer, Incarnate Word High School, San Antonio, Texas

13. EXPRESS YOURSELF.

Along the lines of finding your own style is using it to express yourself and your many moods. Don't let what you think is your "style" limit you, either. Just because you feel like wearing conservative khakis from

Old Navy on Monday doesn't mean you can't be seen in black vinyl pants from Thrift Town on Tuesday. Let your mood and your personality shine through in your outfits. Keep in mind, however, that the way you dress can and will lead people to make judgments about you. Check yourself if the way people are seeing you isn't the way you are seeing yourself. If you are just wearing the patent leather miniskirt because you were feeling glam, but you get nasty looks from girlfriends and you come home with drool all over, you have to decide if this is how you want to portray yourself. Clothes should boost your confidence, not destroy your self-respect.

14. MAKE YOUR OWN RULES.

Basically, there really are no specific rules. In today's fashion world, almost any hemline, style, and color is acceptable, which makes it even easier to find an outfit that looks good on you, because any that you like will be in style. If you like the way something looks and you are comfortable wearing it, go for it.

On that note, let these tips be a loose basis for solving all your fashion woes. Most importantly, if remember to be yourself, you can't go wrong. Good luck, and happy shopping!

I'll watch TV tonight - then finish all my homework in a frenzy BEFORE CLASS!

CHAPTER 21

Time Management

One of the best things about high school is that you can get involved in so many different activities. No matter what your interests are, high school can provide a fun and risk-free environment to try out many new things. In fact, so many options will become available to you that you will quickly realize that you cannot be involved in *everything*. Overloading can lead to major stress sessions, not to mention having a bad impact on schoolwork. When your four years are over, you will want to feel satisfied that you chose just the right way to spend your time, but to do that you must acquire time-management skills. This chapter will help you decide what your best options are while still being both involved and sane.

> *Coming into high school, I was really involved in a lot of different kinds of activities: soccer, field hockey, basketball, theater, singing, playing violin and piano, and school, not to mention time spent with friends and family. All were really important to me, and I didn't want to give up any activities. But coming into high school upset the balance of time I spent on each activity, and I found myself spending more time on schoolwork and showing up to music lessons without having practiced at all in the past week. I had to give up piano and violin lessons, which I had been taking since kindergarten. I just knew that the best thing for my future was to postpone my lessons until I could afford the time.*
>
> —MERRITT, HERITAGE HIGH SCHOOL, LITTLETON, COLORADO

Prioritize!

Prioritizing is going to be the key to managing your time. You can't do everything, so you need to decide what things you most want or need to spend time doing. Prioritizing should extend to many parts of your life, whether it be choosing what activities to participate in or which homework assignment to tackle first. Prioritizing occurs on many levels, which are all important because your time is priceless.

1. Use prioritizing to tackle homework hassles.

Often, when you find yourself faced with a scary amount of homework, you will want to moan and groan instead of getting to work in the most efficient manner. Most of us have sat at our desks staring at the reams of paper and stacks of books and wondered how we would get everything done. This phenomenon is called the "I hate my teachers for doing this to me stage," and it can get ugly. You must get a grip, however, and get to work. The key to tackling these seemingly impossible tasks is to take them one step at a time. Make a mental picture of your *actual* workload. The word *actual* is very important here. Often, you will think that you have much more work to do than you actually do. Once you have a firm grasp of the work that needs to be done, you can decide which task requires the most immediate attention.

- First of all, you should approximate how much time it will take for each assignment. If it adds up to more time than you have, you need to prioritize.

- Next, decide which work is easy, and leave that until last (it'll be much harder to think clearly at 2 a.m.).

- If your assignments have different due dates, you should work on the one that is due the soonest.

- Also, even though it is a little bit scary, you really should work first on homework from the subject that you are getting the worst grade in at the present time. If you put the same effort into all your classes, you will only continue to do poorly in that class. To bring it up, you need to give more effort to your hardest subject.

Effectively using your time will definitely reduce your stress level and help you do well in school.

2. MAKE A MENTAL SCHEDULE.

> *I mentally plan out what I have to do. I think to myself, "I have to do this and this and this, and it is going to take me this long." When things come up, I have to revise my plans and take into account the other things I have to do. I make two plans. The first is a long-term plan I come up with at the beginning of the week, taking into account everything I know I have to do. The second is a daily plan. I think about what has to be done for the day. By the end of the day, I am happy I got everything done and begin to plan for the new work I have.*
>
> —NICK, BELLEVUE HIGH SCHOOL, BELLEVUE, WASHINGTON

The second key to effective time management is possessing the ability to plan your day. This skill of "mental-scheduling" can save you from coming to a class unprepared or missing an important practice or meeting. This method requires very little effort and can be done anywhere at any time. Many people find the best time to begin thinking about their day is when they hit the shower in the morning. Shower time is otherwise wasted time and can be used productively. Start with your first-period class and work your way through the day, asking yourself if everything is ready for those classes. If you realize you haven't finished an assignment or studied for a test, it is much better to know before school, when you may have a few extra minutes, than when you walk into math class and the teacher calls for your incomplete assignment. As your day progresses, continue to think about your remaining classes. Think about whether you have any activities or sports after school so that you can plan accordingly. If tennis practice is right after school, don't tell your best friend that you can work on a history project at the same time.

Making this mental picture will permit you to do two things: First, you will have a clearer sense of what needs to be done for the day; second, you can figure how much time you will have available to get work done in the evening. Mental scheduling is a quick, easy, and effective way to plan your day and complete all your assignments.

3. MAXIMIZE WOULD-BE WASTED TIME.

The third step in effective time management involves making productive use out of unused time. Take a glance at your day, and as hectic as it may seem, you should begin to notice wasted time. Wasted time is any time that you aren't getting something done. This can include gaps in the period when the teacher isn't teaching, extra time during lunch, time between school and sports practice, or time when you are waiting to get a ride. These are perfect opportunities to whip out your notebook and check off some of the little daily assignments you need to do anyway. This also is a good time to do work because it may rank low on your priority list for the evening if you have other, more important work to do. Finish the math page you started in class or the history matching exercise. Busy-work can be knocked off in no time, with very little effort, without wasting time you need to spend on bigger assignments. This tip requires a little more effort than some of the others, but it pays tremendous dividends in time saved to do other work.

4. YOUR DAY PLANNER IS YOUR FRIEND.

Making use of a calendar, organizer, or day planner is one of the easiest ways to manage time, keep track of assignments, and remain stress-free. Most planners are inexpensive, simple to use, and effective. Any basic planner will work. For $10 or less, you should be able to find a basic planner with ample space to record all assignments, activities, and extracurricular activities. The planner can be your most useful tool in time management if it is used effectively. Two steps are required for the planner to work:

- The first step is to write down the assignment as soon as the teacher gives it.

- The second step is to look at your planner when you are home to see what needs to be done.

The planner is no good if you don't follow both steps. Many people like to write down their assignments in a blank, lined notebook. This isn't always as effective, however, because it is more difficult to glance quickly at what work needs to be done for each class. The most important thing to remember is that the planner is only as good as the entries you make in it and can be effective only when you read the entries. Using a paper clip to pull back the old pages can make it much simpler to find the current date and quickly jot down a note.

5. USE CHECKLISTS TO SUPPLEMENT PRIORITIZING.

When your homework appears to be never ending, make a clear list outlining your plan of attack. After you decide which items are the most important, number and write them on a lined sheet of paper. In the margin at the left of each number, make a small square. You will put a check mark in the square when you complete that assignment. Making a list provides you with a sense of direction. You would never want to drive across the country without a roadmap; a checklist can serve as your roadmap, showing you a clear path to completion.

6. START WORKING ON LONG-TERM HOMEWORK AS SOON AS IT IS ASSIGNED.

> *I do all my work when it is first assigned. That way, when other things come up, I can be prepared to do them because all my work is done.*
>
> —NATHANIEL, MERCER ISLAND HIGH SCHOOL, MERCER ISLAND, WASHINGTON

Getting your work done when it is assigned is great advice because it will save you time and energy and will prevent untold amounts of stress. As great as this may sound, however, the truth is that very few people possess the motivation required to finish an assignment two weeks before it is due. Although not everyone has super study habits, it is very possible—and easy—to begin working on an assignment well before the deadline.

Start by coming up with a plan of how you are going to complete the assignment. If you know that you will be working on it up until the last minute, create the necessary foundation to guide you. If your English teacher gives you three weeks to write an essay, start well in advance writing a little bit every day. Chip away at it, like they say, one step at a time. In many cases, your work will be better if you plan ahead because you are not obligated to work quickly.

7. DON'T PROCRASTINATE.

Waiting until the last minute is one of the biggest (and by far the most common) mistakes you can make in high school. Don't force yourself to stay up until 3:00 in the morning the day your project is due. Don't wait until the last minute to study for your biology exam. If you are told you will be having a test in four days, begin preparing from the first day you hear the news. If a project is assigned, gather as much information as you can during the first few days. As much as you probably hate wasting your time on something that isn't due the next day, you'll benefit in the long run.

My first major test in high school happened to be in one of my hardest classes: biology. The teacher warned us of the test in plenty of time for me to accomplish all the studying I would need. When my teacher gave us study sheets, I was grateful that she had provided an outline for us to study from. I then put the sheet away, thinking, "I'll pull it out when the test date comes closer." So I took my time and let a week pass without even glancing at the fluorescent green sheet. I had four more days to go, then three, and then two. Every day I would plan to study and end up putting it off until the next day, when I would have more time or when my favorite TV show wasn't on. On the night before the big test, I stayed up really late, feeling anxious and unprepared, with only a bottomless cup of coffee to console me. Although I earned an average test grade, I know I could have done much better if I had used the time the teacher had given me. It took this experience, and a few more like it, for me to come to the conclusion

> *that tests are much easier to study for by breaking the*
> *studying into smaller components over a number of*
> *days rather than trying to cram the night before a test.*
>
> —Alyssa, Mercer Island High School, Mercer Island,
> Washington

8. Take advantage of class time.

In the same way you use down time to your advantage, make productive use of class time. An additional benefit to working in class is that everyone around you is working on the same material and can help if you come across a problem. Many students simply waste work time in class by saying, "I'll do it at home." However, quite often other assignments or obligations come up, and if you get the work done, you'll be free to devote your time elsewhere (maybe even to doing something fun, such as watching your favorite TV program or shooting hoops).

Being able to ask the teacher for help also can aid you in better understanding the work so that you don't waste precious work time struggling with concepts you cannot comprehend. Class time is a gift from your teacher and should be used to your benefit. When you finish all the work your teacher gives you, catch up on work or studying for another class. Often, a quick refresher the period before a test can jump-start your brain and give you a competitive edge for the upcoming test.

9. Choose your extracurricular activities carefully.

> *High school is great because so many opportunities*
> *will present themselves. You should expose yourself to*
> *as many different options as are possible early on so*
> *that you begin to discover which activities you love*
> *and which you could live without. Don't pursue the*
> *activities you don't love. Not only do you not enjoy*
> *them, but this is poor time management and wastes*
> *precious hours. However, sometimes participating in*

> *activities can be a blessing in disguise, forcing you to become more organized to account for your busier schedule. When I was inactive, my time-management skills were poor. But when I became involved in piano and tennis, I was forced to become better organized; because of it, I flourished academically.*
>
> —Ajay, Mercer Island High School, Mercer Island, Washington

Not everyone will see the same immediate results Ajay did. Many people struggle to keep ahead of schoolwork and to maintain friendships while participating in activities. For most of these people, it takes a little while to develop the study habits necessary to participate while still maintaining good grades and sustaining friendships.

> *When I took up varsity crew, I had no idea how big a time commitment it would be. I knew I needed to re-prioritize my schedule so as to not fail all my classes. At first, my schedule was so stressful that after crew and student council meetings, I would study until the wee hours. At this point, I was surviving only on caffeine and tried to convince myself that every day was Friday to motivate myself to get out of bed. This had put a definite strain on my social life. Fortunately, after a few weeks, I got into the routine and found myself making the most out of every minute of free time. Now my organizational skills are much improved and I can balance school, crew, and friends.*
>
> —Jennifer, Mercer Island High School, Mercer Island, Washington

10. Go for balance.

As great as extracurricular activities can be in helping you organize, make sure you maintain a proper balance of activities, studying, and down time. This balance can vary from person to person: Some people are busy from the moment they wake up until the moment their head hits the pillow. They couldn't function any other way. We all know that superhero who plays soccer, wrestles, plays in the jazz band and the wind ensemble, coaches youth soccer, and is an active Boy Scout and Natural Helper while taking honors classes that require multiple books to be read each week. Most people cannot keep up with such a hectic pace. Still, you can use some of the same techniques in your life. Simply put, if you love participating in something, you can coordinate everything else to work around it. You just have to find the balance that is right for you. Experiment, don't be afraid to change the way you work, and discover how much is too much for you and build off of that. Be sure to take advantage of the benefits of being active, and permit yourself to utilize various time-management techniques to build your schedule around activities you love.

11. Use multiple time-management techniques, and plan for the long term.

Major assignments can be the ones that cause you the most stress. The importance of planning ahead and thinking long term cannot be underestimated. Many tools used in conjunction with each other can improve long-term planning. Calendars are a perfect way to take a quick glance at where you are and where you should be going. Mental planning also should be utilized to keep you mindful of areas that require your attention. Planning ahead for big assignments can prevent massive hysteria the day before the essay is due.

Successful organization begins with long-term planning. Joining clubs or committing to play a sport requires you to make long-term commitments. Before joining, ask yourself these questions, keeping in mind you are not just answering for the next week or two, but for the entire duration of the program.

- Are you really committed to rowing two-and-a-half hours a day for the next three months?

- Will you get all your work done?

- Will it impede on your social life?

- Does it conflict with any prior commitments you have?
- Can you stand to lose flexibility in your schedule?

If you answer no to any of these questions, you should reconsider your original decision. Asking these questions is just one of the many ways you can think long term and save yourself from stress and unneeded aggravation down the road.

JUST GO FOR IT!

> *Enjoying high school is much like skiing: To have fun, you have to realize that you're never going to be in complete control. Work hard and do your best, and let the rest fall into place. Then just sit back and enjoy the ride.*
>
> —CONNIE, MERCER ISLAND HIGH SCHOOL, MERCER ISLAND, WASHINGTON

The best time-management techniques in the world can't guarantee that you will complete every assignment on time, ace every test, and receive A's in all your classes. These techniques can only guide you in the right direction and provide you with a few helpful hints on ways to succeed. They are only as good as you make them. Day planners don't do your assignments for you. When used effectively, however, they can aid in your academic success.

Do the best you can, and then be happy with the results. There is a lot more to life than homework, tests, and soccer games—as if we needed to remind you.

CHAPTER 22

Dealing with Parents

> *I was at a party one night toward the end of the school year. I was planning to take the SAT the next day, but I felt like I needed to just unwind and hang out with my friends for a while. I called home to check in and my parents told me that I had to be home by 11 p.m. I was so ticked—I usually didn't have a set curfew, and my parents had always been really trusting. They said that I needed to get a good night's sleep, though, and at the time I thought they were being the most irrational people on earth. Looking back on it, I can see that they were definitely right—although I'd never acknowledge that to them!*
>
> —DAN, HERITAGE HIGH SCHOOL, LITTLETON, COLORADO

Parents—they're the most important (and sometimes the most difficult) people in your life. They raise you, they love you, they brag to their friends about you, and they probably bug you. But hey, that's life, and you're going to have to work out some system of communication during your high school years.

High school is when you get more freedom than ever before. You're likely to lose this newfound freedom, however, if you break your parents' trust. Like it or not, your social life depends on keeping a healthy relationship with your parents.

Leaving the House: How to Keep Both Parties Happy

Your social schedule can be a very touchy subject, and one over which many tears have been shed. The key is communication and compromise. If you follow these hints, you are much more likely to be able to do the things you want and stay on speaking terms with the 'rents.

1. Respect each other.

Even if they seem totally unfair, try to respect your parents' views— and get them to respect yours. This means that when they tell you that you can't go to that party, you don't scream obscenities and then sneak out anyway. They have reasons for their decisions, and if you have a good reason for why you disagree, then there's nothing wrong with talking to them coolly about it. Perhaps there's a piece of information they don't know about your evening. Or, if your friend's parents are going to be home, then you could suggest that they call your friend's house. If it's homework they're worried about, then maybe you could suggest a schedule for finishing your homework over the rest of the weekend.

2. Know when to give up.

If you can tell it's an absolute no, then don't push it. If you know when to give in, you can save yourself time and maybe catch a break the next time. Arguing over a lost cause makes them listen less when you do have a legitimate claim.

3. Be open to compromises.

Often, if you are both willing to compromise, you both end up satisfied. Just stay reasonable and listen to your parents' reasons; you can usually work something out. If you're still trying to compromise and your parents have laid down the rule already, then see the previous tip.

> *Often, I'll want to go to a football game or something during the week, and even though I'm not supposed to go out on school nights, I can compromise with my*

> *parents. Sometimes I can work something out, such*
> *as finishing my homework first and then going out*
> *for an hour, or something.*
>
> —Peter, Heritage High School, Littleton, Colorado

4. Earn and keep their trust.

When you climb out the window to get to that forbidden party, it might not seem like a big deal. In fact, you might even feel self-righteous. However, by doing something like climbing out of your window, you are betraying your parents' trust. If you get caught, it's incredibly difficult to earn that trust back. Use good judgment. That party had better be well worth losing your parents' respect.

> *One time I told my parents that I was just going to a*
> *friend's house, but I ended up stopping at a party first.*
> *When I didn't show up at my friend's house on time,*
> *she called my parents, and they got all worried—it*
> *was a really big deal, bigger than I thought. Now I*
> *always keep in touch, just to be sure, but they still*
> *don't trust me as much.*
>
> —Eloise, SCECGS, Sydney, Australia

Unfortunately for us, parents are usually smarter than we think. When your mom is sitting on your bed waiting for you to return, your social life has dark clouds of gloom hanging over it for the next decade or so. Of course, it's your decision how you handle disagreements with parents. Remember, though, that as much as high school can mean newfound freedom, it can also mean that your room becomes county jail and your parents become the wardens, if you're not careful.

WHEN YOU JUST DID SOMETHING THAT WILL *NOT* MAKE THEM PROUD

1. BE HONEST.

We know it's hard at times to tell your parents stuff, but they are actually amazingly well-informed most of the time. And especially if you know that they are going to find out later, it's *much* better that they hear it from you than from friends, teachers, or policemen. We are not suggesting that you tell your mom *everything*—but it's generally a good idea to be open from the start. So, you don't have to tell your parents who you think is really fine, but you can't hide that failing grade in chemistry or the 12 parking tickets forever.

> *One time I ditched a class and got caught, and since the school didn't call my mom, I thought I could just let it pass. She ended up finding out from my friend's mom, and it turned into a much bigger deal because she was disappointed that I wasn't honest with her.*
>
> —MERRITT, HERITAGE HIGH SCHOOL, LITTLETON, COLORADO

Every once in a while, we run into situations that we just don't know how to handle. Sometimes these situations can be dangerous, such as if you heard a kid at school talking about suicide, or if you're worried that one of your friends has a drug problem. It's okay to need help dealing with these things, and parents are usually a great source of advice. The nice thing about parents is that 99 percent of the time, their first loyalty is going to be to you. That means that they will do their best to make sure that you are protected from whatever is going on. If there's something serious going on, ask your mom or dad (or aunt, uncle, grandparent, and so on) if you can talk about it. They will understand your concerns, and chances are they'll know what the right course of action.

Even if it's just about your date to the dance (parents love living vicariously through their children) or the test you failed, do the best you can to be open with your parents—it'll make for a better relationship between you and will build their trust in you.

2. REMEMBER THAT THEY LOVE YOU.

No matter how upset or disappointed they might act, never forget that your parents love you pretty much no matter what, and that any decisions they make are (theoretically) with your best interests at heart. Try to be forgiving—parents are people, too. They make mistakes, but they really do want the best for you.

"UM, MOM, I FLUNKED MATH . . . "

One of the hardest subjects to discuss with parents is grades. Sure, it's all fine when you're getting straight A's, but we all know what it feels like to see red ink all over a test. When you get a bad grade on a test or for a class in general, your parents will probably want to know about it. And as hard as it is to tell them, it's part of keeping up a good relationship. Who knows? They might be in a position to help.

Often, there's a logical reason for a disappointing grade, and parents will be more understanding if they know that it isn't just because you're not trying. Maybe you need an algebra review course, or maybe you need to cut down on your extracurricular activities. Whatever the reason, you should discuss it with your parents *before* they get that scary report card. If they are prepared, they will be much more understanding.

BASIC TIPS FOR FORMING A GOOD RELATIONSHIP WITH THE 'RENTS

1. APPRECIATE THEM (AND TELL THEM SO!).

Okay, so they're not always perfect, but they're doing their best, and they really are doing a lot for you. Every time your dad drives you to soccer practice, he is sacrificing his time. When your mom does a load of laundry, when your dad takes you shoe shopping . . . there are so many sacrifices parents make that we just take them for granted. So, even if your mom tries to clean your room and ends up throwing away your favorite pair of green socks, keep in mind that she is trying to show her love by being helpful. And don't hesitate to tell your parents how much you appreciate everything, either. It'll make their day and put some points in your bank account.

2. TALK TO YOUR PARENTS.

Your parents were teenagers, too, and though times have changed, people haven't changed that much. Your parents have probably faced some of the same problems you are facing. You have so many opportunities to talk to them, whether it's in the car, at the dinner table, or when you come into their room after you get back from a friend's house. If you know and understand your parents better, you will not only have better communication, but you'll find that you have fewer disagreements and misunderstandings.

3. MAKE TIME FOR THEM.

There's nothing that makes a parent feel better than having one of their kids say, "Hey, Mom, I was wondering if you'd like to go catch the matinee of that new movie tomorrow." Or, "Dad, do you want to go play some catch?" Even a short activity together every once in a while can make a huge difference in your relationship.

4. OFFER TO HELP OUT.

Running a household takes a ton of work, and chances are that your parents already have another job during the day. Anything you can do to help out around the house—raking leaves, doing dishes, vacuuming the family room—will be greatly appreciated. Rumor has it that parents who see their kids taking part in keeping up the house are much more likely to let them go out and have a good time with their friends.

REMEMBERING WHAT'S IMPORTANT

Every parent is different, just as every kid is. There are no magical rules that work for every parent—if there were, we wouldn't need to include this chapter. The best advice is to remember that everyone is human and that they're doing their best. Your relationship with your parents will have ups and downs. If you communicate and earn their trust, however, the ups should outnumber the downs.

CHAPTER 23

Nutrition: Eating Right and Living Right in High School

> *It's 6:00 in the morning. Once I finally manage to get myself out of bed, I work my way across the hall, toward the bathroom. After I take a shower and get dressed, I go downstairs to pack up all my schoolbooks. Ready to fight the morning traffic, I then rush out of the house. I don't bother to make my lunch or eat—I am not a morning person. Waking up is a chore for me, something that takes effort. I know that I should eat before school and not skip the "most important meal of the day." But there's just no time!*
>
> —ANNIE, MERCER ISLAND HIGH SCHOOL,
> MERCER ISLAND, WASHINGTON

Does the story above sound familiar? High school is more action packed than most Sly Stallone movies, and all too often we find ourselves wrapped up in classes, homework, rehearsals, practices, meetings, work, and on and on. But it's important to remember that to take advantage of everything that an active high school life offers, you have to take care of yourself and make sure that you keep up your energy so that you can tackle the hectic life of a high-schooler.

Eleven Rules for a Healthy Lifestyle

1. Start your morning off with a good breakfast.

Eating a breakfast is a must! Believe it or not, one day of high school can be draining on your body. The best way to prevent exhaustion during the day is to start it out right. You can eat practically anything for breakfast: a piece of fruit, slice of cold pizza, or cereal. You can even go all out and feast on a plate full of bacon, scrambled eggs, and hash browns with a stack of blueberry pancakes on the side.

If you don't have time to eat your breakfast at home, then take it to go. While you're walking to your bus stop, munch on some raspberry breakfast bars or cocoa puffs; you never want to leave home feeling hungry. It's hard to concentrate in Spanish class when all you can think about is French toast.

2. Eat a variety of foods.

A variety of foods is loaded with vitamins and minerals necessary for maintaining a healthy body. You'll often find yourself eating the same types of foods (potato chips, cookies, soda) and not realize that your diet is lacking important nutrients. By eating a variety of foods, you'll have a more balanced diet and be able to function efficiently. Also, drinking eight glasses of milk every day isn't the only way to satisfy your daily calcium requirements. You can eat cheese, yogurt, ice cream, or almost any kind of leafy green vegetable.

Eating a balanced diet shouldn't be painful. The great thing about high school is that there will always be different kinds of foods available at your convenience. Just make sure that you eat from a wide range of foods that give you essential nutrients so that you don't suffer from malnutrition.

If you are a vegetarian, try to balance your diet with protein. Protein can be found in legumes, tofu, and certain vegetables such as spinach.

Also try to eat something from the major food groups during each day. You probably can find something you like in each one. Following are some recommendations for healthy eating on a daily basis.

- Bread, cereal, rice, and pasta (6 to 11 servings)
- Fruits (2 to 4 servings)
- Vegetables (3 to 5 servings)
- Meat, poultry, eggs, nuts, fish, and dry beans (2 to 3 servings)
- Milk, yogurt, and cheese (2 to 3 servings)
- Fats, oils, and sweets (use sparingly)

The U.S. Department of Agriculture and Department of Health and Human Services publish dietary guidelines to advise all Americans of how to eat healthy. These guidelines apply to teenagers as well as adults:

- Eat a variety of foods.
- Use sugars only in moderation.
- Use salt and sodium only in moderation.
- Eat plenty of vegetables, fruits, and grain products.
- Eat foods that are low in fat, saturated fat, and cholesterol.
- Stay healthy by balancing food eaten with regular exercise.

---

3. EAT HIGH-ENERGY FOODS.

When there's only three seconds left on the shot clock and you're team is down by two points, you don't want to be the one stuck on the bench because you didn't have enough stamina to finish the game. You should have known that scarfing down that double-filled cream puff before the game wasn't going to give you the energy you needed to score the three-pointer at the buzzer to win the game. Fruits, water, juice, or energy bars would've done better for you.

Even if you're not a superstar athlete, you still need to eat high-energy foods to get through the day. Carbohydrates such as pasta, rice, and bread will give you more energy than chocolate-covered donuts and gummy bears.

> *My coach always stresses nutrition to us. The night before each football game, he invites just about the whole team to his house for a pasta and salad dinner. The pasta contains complex carbohydrates, which makes it a key energy food. We also drink as much water as we can for an ample amount of hydration. The following day we are all energized and set to go for the game.*
>
> —CASEY ROSE, MILILANI HIGH SCHOOL, MILILANI, HAWAII

4. EAT BECAUSE YOU'RE HUNGRY, NOT JUST BECAUSE YOU'RE STRESSED OUT OR DEPRESSED.

Listen to your stomach. When it's hungry, eat. When it's not hungry, don't eat. All too often students will start gaining weight because they eat whenever they feel stressed out. You should know when to stop eating—hint: it's when you're full. Food shouldn't be something you turn to when you're stressed out or depressed. So if you just got rejected by your long-time crush and find yourself sprawled across the couch, watching the old movie marathon and finishing that bucket of double-fudge ice cream, snap out of it! You shouldn't abuse food like that, because even though it can do a lot of things, it can't solve your problems. If you eat only when you're hungry, chances are you won't ever feel the need to diet.

5. CUSTOMIZE EATING TO YOUR OWN BODY.

You must learn how to customize eating to your own body. If you're the type who gets hungry easily, bring snacks to school. You should pack an extra sack of food or save food from lunch so that you won't feel hungry later in the day. After-school activities can last for hours, even up until dinnertime. You don't want to be stuck at school without enough food. You should know how your body functions so that you can better prepare yourself for whatever you plan on doing.

> *I have speech team after school almost every day until 5:00 p.m. I eat lunch at noon, so I get really hungry by the end of the day. Once I went without eating anything the entire day, so after speech practice I bought two hot dogs. I felt sick after eating them, though. The following day, I bought myself two lunches at the cafeteria. I learned to never skip lunch and always to make sure that I have enough food for the entire day, including after-school activities.*
>
> —JENNY, BRONX HIGH SCHOOL OF SCIENCE, NEW YORK CITY, NEW YORK

6. DON'T BE A VICTIM OF JUNK FOOD.

Don't be a slave to the dreaded vending machine monster. You have to fight the urge. For the most part, the foods in the vending machines shouldn't even be called foods—they are unhealthy and don't give you enough energy to get through the day. Sure, the candy bars are yummy and tempting, but they provide only short-term energy. You definitely cannot substitute your lunch with the foods from the vending machine.

Instead, invest your money in real food. You may not like the cafeteria food, but at least you know that it's the turkey and cheese in the sandwich, not the partially hydrogenated polysaccharides in the potato chips that are lining your stomach.

7. DON'T EAT LUNCH ON THE RUN.

When you're eating, enjoy yourself. Don't rob yourself of lunch, the best period of the day. Lunch will be your longest break from having to deal with school, and it is the only time you can just relax and hang out with your friends. Lunchtime is probably the most underrated aspect of high school. If you eat on the run, you'll be depriving yourself of the time you could've spent taking a rest from your hectic schedule. You'll also have to deal with the heartburn and upset stomach afterward.

8. BRING A SACK LUNCH.

Believe it or not, you won't be made fun of for bringing your sack lunch. (I don't think we're in middle school anymore, Toto.) Packing a sack lunch doesn't take that much time in the morning, and the big plus is that you can put whatever you want in it. Bringing your lunch to school is not only convenient, but it's a lot cheaper, too. If you buy lunch from the cafeteria, expect to spend at least $2 to $3 per day for a good meal and a drink. So, either bring a sack lunch or be prepared for the great cafeteria food scam.

9. FIND A BALANCE BETWEEN PROPER DIET AND EXERCISE.

Proper diet and exercise go hand in hand. Your best bet is to stick to a reasonable diet and exercise plan. Remember that dieting doesn't necessarily mean going on a strict diet; it simply refers to regulating what you put in your mouth. Don't think that you have to drastically cut down on the amount of food you eat or limit your diet to just carrot sticks and water, because sometimes your body needs fat as an essential nutrient.

Eating healthy foods won't always make you feel healthy, though. That's why it is important to exercise. You should find the right balance between the foods you eat and how much you exercise for your own body. Don't try to outdo yourself, though. It's not a good idea to force your body to run 6 miles for exercise one day if you haven't run in a while. Try to build up your endurance by taking it step by step. Run $1/2$ mile this week and 1 mile the next. Let your body get used to the running. If you're not fond of running, you can apply this method to any other sport or kind of exercise.

Keep in mind that too much exercise is stressful for your body. You should know how much exercise and what kind of diet your body can handle, which is also why you should stay away from weird diets you hear about. Let's face it, those diets usually never work, and if they do happen to yield results, it's only in the beginning of the diet for a short period of time. Weird diets can be dangerous: Just eating an apple or a diet pill a day will not give your body the nutrients it needs. Exercising for 10 hours straight will not make you fit, either. (But it will make you weak.) For some, maintaining the proper diet and exercise plan comes naturally. For others, it is a hard and overwhelming task.

Crash diets can be very dangerous and can tax your energy. If you feel that you need to diet, you might want to talk it over with your parents or someone else who can offer advice. There are ways to manage your eating habits safely, and it might help if you get advice before going it on your own.

After hundreds of dollars spent on Jenny Craig and Weight Watchers for months on end, my mother and I were sadly forced to resort to the method of self-discipline as our battle plan for weight-loss. The actual process of dieting by self-discipline is an act of insanity, which I believe is achieved only by those who sell their souls to Richard Simmons.

A friend sent me a two-page recipe for what is simply called, "The Seven-Day Diet Soup," and consists of cabbage, tomatoes, and beef broth boiled to a pulp. At the end of the recipe read an explanation for the soup, made primarily for obese, high-risk heart surgery patients who need to lose 10 to 17 pounds the week previous to their surgery. Although I wasn't an obese heart surgery patient lying weak in my hospital bed, I thought I'd give "The Diet Soup" a try. After the first day, I had eaten what I thought to be a gallon of mushy brown slop, but I remained optimistic about the idea. The second day yielded a more severe reaction, and I began to tire of the dreaded soup sitting innocently atop the stove. On the fifth day of what I refer to now as "The Seven-Day Starve," I had never craved a slice of Wonderbread so greatly in all my 17 years. I had lost 3 pounds total over the five days, and I realized that I was not at all near the estimated 10 supposedly lost in that amount of time. On the sixth day, I succumbed to the pressures of all the Oreo cookies, extra-cheesy Doritos, and cookie-dough ice cream that

> *hollered my name from the cupboards. "The Seven-Day Diet Soup" taught me the valuable lesson that my self-discipline needs to be fine-tuned, or else I'm going back to Weight Watchers to join my sympathizers.*
>
> —OLIVIA, SHORECREST HIGH SCHOOL, SEATTLE, WASHINGTON

10. DON'T ABUSE YOUR SACRED SLEEPING TIME.

It's midnight. You have a project on all the 400-plus functions of the liver due the next day for biology, and you've only written up to the 157th function. But you're really tired because you've been working on homework for your five other classes ever since you got back from gymnastics practice. What should you do? For freshmen, the lack of sleep will be a rude awakening. It is recommended that you get at least seven to eight hours of sleep a day. But how much you sleep, as with how much you eat and exercise, really depends on you. By senior year, if you're taking more AP and honors courses than you can handle, you will appreciate the beauty of sleep. If you're dozing off in classes, or whenever you get home the only thing you look forward to is being in your warm, cozy bed, then you know you're not getting enough sleep.

Your body appreciates being able to depend on getting sleep when it needs it. Go to bed at a regular time so that your body can adjust to a sleeping pattern. Don't worry if you need more sleep than your friends do: The hours of sleep a person needs can vary. So, if you can't seem to stay awake and still have unfinished homework, just go to bed!

You can always work ahead if you know that next week you'll be swamped with projects, or tell your teacher the situation and that you need an extension. Your teacher would rather you turn in a well-written report than a poorly written one caked with dried slobber.

11. MAXIMIZE YOUR SLEEPING TIME.

An effective way to maximize your sleeping time is to take short naps. Most likely, you'll feel tired when you come home from school. Don't be reluctant to take a nap. If you try to do homework or read while you're tired, then forget it—you're not going to get much done.

The worst thing you can do is waste your time and energy trying to stay awake. Naps come in handy because sometimes you didn't have a good night's sleep the night before or just feel more drained out from school. If you feel a bit groggy after waking up, hop in the shower for five minutes and you'll feel reinvigorated.

I take naps almost every day. Ever since junior year, my body has developed a pattern that allows me to take naps after school. The only problem is, when season starts, I have to fight the urge to sleep! Otherwise, taking power naps has helped me regenerate enough energy to finish my homework and make the most out of my time.

—Annie, Mercer Island High School, Mercer Island, Washington

Eating Disorders

More than 2 million Americans—mostly women and girls—suffer from eating disorders. Eating disorders involve obsessions with food and body weight. The three major types are *anorexia nervosa, bulimia nervosa,* and *binge-eating disorder.*

One in every 150 teenage girls in the United States suffers from anorexia nervosa. A person suffering from this condition will usually over-exercise, starve oneself, and feel fat even though he or she is very thin. A person affected by bulimia nervosa may be caught in the cycle of bingeing and purging. Bingeing occurs when a person eats a large amount of food in a short amount of time. After bingeing, a bulimic person will purge by vomiting or taking laxatives. The only difference in the binge-eating disorder is that the person does not purge after bingeing.

Eating disorders can cause both emotional and physical problems and can be caused by several factors:

- The constant need for control and to be perfect
- Low self-esteem in general
- Negative body image because of the way American culture views thinness

The factors that lead to eating disorders are not flaws in the people themselves; they are usually the result of external pressures.

SOME THINGS TO REMEMBER ABOUT EATING DISORDERS

1. EVERYONE'S BODY IS DIFFERENT.

Remember that a lot of what we look like is determined by factors outside our control. Some people have super-high metabolisms, while others don't. But when it comes down to it, real people like people for their hearts, not their metabolisms.

> *Entering high school can be stressful on both your mind and your body. You'll be exposed to all different kinds of people of different backgrounds and shapes and sizes. You probably already understand that everyone is different. Well, the body is no exception. Who knows? Your best friend might be 10 inches taller than you! Since most of us are still growing, the beginning years of high school can be an awkward and difficult period. Just hang in there and stay true to yourself. Don't trick yourself into thinking that by changing your appearance, you'll be able to build more trustworthy relationships. When you move up to high school, don't change for others. The people who truly are interested in you will like you for who you are and not what you try to be. Eat healthy and get exercise because it makes you feel good, not because you think it makes others like you.*
>
> —Menulique, Center Senior High School, Kansas City, Missouri

2. Know the symptoms.

The best thing you can do for yourself is to know the symptoms of eating disorders and hopefully catch yourself if you start exhibiting any of the signs.

These signs generally indicate anorexia nervosa:

- Complaining about one's body all the time
- Becoming very thin and weak
- Growing fine hair on arms and legs
- Having dry skin and hair
- Having brittle nails and swollen joints
- Constantly feeling cold
- Hiding one's body in baggy clothes
- Stopping menstruation

The symptoms of bulimia nervosa include these:

- Fluctuating significantly in weight
- Not changing in body weight despite constant eating
- Developing a chronic sore throat
- Suffering from bloating or other digestive problems
- Misusing diuretics or laxatives
- Always going to the bathroom after eating
- Having worn-down tooth enamel because of the stomach acids from vomiting
- Having irregular menstrual cycles

These are some symptoms of binge-eating disorder:

- Continuing to eat, even when full
- Gaining weight rapidly
- Feeling guilty after bingeing

The general symptoms of an eating disorder include an obsession with food and denial that anything might be wrong. If you think that you or a friend show the symptoms of an eating disorder, you should seriously consider consulting a doctor. No one can force you to get help, because you must be the one who is willing to seek help. Admitting that you have the problem is the first step. If you have an eating disorder, it's never too late to turn back and seek help—you can be treated.

> *Ever since freshman year, my friend and I were very close. In our junior year, she had to transfer schools, and that's when everything fell apart. Whenever I would talk to her on the phone, she'd talk about how she gained a few pounds. She obsessed about food and she always ate too much. The last time I saw her, I was in shock. She had gone from a size 10 to a size 0 in less than a year. She was initially anorexic; then she became bulimic. I noticed that her teeth were wearing away. That smile of hers I had seen for years had changed. Sometimes we would go out to eat and right after she finished her meal, she would go to the rest room. It was hard seeing her suffer and not being able to say anything. I felt helpless because I couldn't force her to get help; she had to be the one who wanted help. It was like watching someone you really cared about simply waste away.*
>
> —Carolyn, Mercer Island High School, Mercer Island, Washington

3. Help out your friends.

If you think your friend has an eating disorder, you must first realize that no one—including yourself—is to blame. Being angry with yourself or your friend will not help solve the problem. Try to be as supportive as possible. Let your friend know that you are willing to help. Don't act mightier than thou.

You may want to talk to someone you trust about the situation. Eating disorders are serious business and can possibly even be fatal. Don't try to handle the situation all by yourself! Talk to your parents or a counselor about what you might do. Depending on the situation, you might keep the name of your friend confidential (don't go telling all your friends about it) until you find the right person to handle the situation. Better safe than sorry.

Final Thoughts

The bottom line is that you shouldn't sacrifice your health just to impress others or "make the grade." Your health—which includes the proper diet, exercise, and amount of sleep—should definitely be a priority. You should never jeopardize your health for anything.

Grades are important, but when they come at the expense of your health, they're not worth it. Take care of your body; it's the only one you've got.

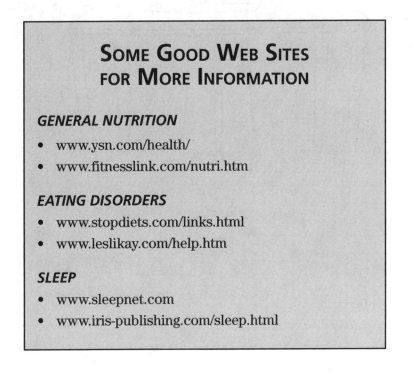

Some Good Web Sites for More Information

GENERAL NUTRITION

- www.ysn.com/health/
- www.fitnesslink.com/nutri.htm

EATING DISORDERS

- www.stopdiets.com/links.html
- www.leslikay.com/help.htm

SLEEP

- www.sleepnet.com
- www.iris-publishing.com/sleep.html

CHAPTER 24

Preparing for Standardized Tests

May was approaching quickly, and we hadn't even reached World War I in our advanced placement European history class. The AP test was in less than a month, and we still had a century to cover! I was convinced that I wasn't going to do well on the test, and I seriously considered not even taking it. But I was walking around a bookstore one day and saw an entire section devoted to test preparation. Several books were specifically on preparing for the AP European history test. I looked through a couple of them and realized that it wouldn't hurt to give the test a shot. I ended up buying one that had several practice tests as well as some funky little software program that went along with the preparatory book.

The front two-thirds of the book was a summary of European history from 1450 to the present day. The last third of the book had several full-length multiple-choice tests and practice essay questions. The software had additional practice tests and explanations. I read the book's summary of the twentieth century, highlighting important people and events. I also re-read my notes and looked over my tests from the whole year. Then I took a practice test on the computer. For

> *each one I missed, the program gave me a detailed*
> *explanation of why my answer was wrong and*
> *clarified why another answer was right. This really*
> *helped me get used to the types of questions that would*
> *be on the actual test. I also read the essay questions. If*
> *I hadn't procrastinated so much I could've reviewed*
> *more, but the book and software still really helped me*
> *prepare. Without them I don't think I would've scored*
> *well at all.*
>
> —Michael, Free State High School, Lawrence, Kansas

Taking standardized tests is something we'll all have to do at some point in high school. But despite all the rumors, it's not actually that big of a deal. You have numerous ways to study and prepare for these tests, and all that's required is some time and effort. This chapter will focus on four standardized tests in particular: the PSAT, SAT, ACT, and AP examinations.

What Exactly Are These Exams?

Good question. Following is a brief summary of each individual test, just in case you are not familiar with all of them.

THE PSAT (PRELIMINARY SAT)

As its name implies, this is an introductory test for the actual SAT. The types of problems are the same, but the PSAT is much shorter. This test is also called the NMSQT (National Merit Scholarship Qualifying Test) and is used to determine which students should be considered for the National Merit Scholar competition. Like the SAT, the PSAT is divided into a math section and a verbal section. In addition, the PSAT has a writing skills section that was first included in the 1997 test. Each section is worth 80 points, for a total of 240 points. National Merit semi-finalists usually score at or above about 212, but this varies from year to year. Unlike the SAT, this test is not required for college admissions. Consequently, it can be a great help in preparing you for the SAT because it is a low-pressure situation and because your scores can give you an idea of how much more preparing you need to do for the SAT.

THE SAT (SCHOLASTIC APTITUDE TEST)

This is probably the most common and well-known of the four tests. The SAT is divided into two sections: a math section and a verbal section. 1600 points are possible on the test, 800 from each section. This test is required by many colleges for admission, but very few have a cut-off score or minimum score required for acceptance.

THE ACT (AMERICAN COLLEGE TESTING PROGRAM)

The ACT is divided into four sections: an English section, a math section, a reading section, and a science reasoning section. A score of 1 to 36 is given for each section, as is an overall composite score. The ACT is required by some colleges for admission (usually by schools west of the Mississippi). It's similar to the SAT, but the verbal sections are slightly different and the math on the ACT can be a little more difficult.

AP (ADVANCED PLACEMENT) EXAMINATIONS

AP tests are administered by the College Board and focus on a single subject. There are AP tests in history, science, English, art, and foreign languages, to name a few. Most high schools offer AP classes during the year. These are high school courses taught at the college level designed to help prepare you for the AP test. The format of the AP test varies slightly, depending on the subject, but it generally consists of a multiple-choice section and an essay section. Scores are given on a scale of 1 to 5, with 5 being the best. Most colleges award credit for scores of 4 or 5, and some even give credit for a 3. Each AP test costs around $70, which at first sounds pretty expensive. But consider that by doing well you could receive college credit; then you wouldn't have to take that class in college, which would definitely be more expensive.

Taking the Tests Without the Stress

One of the biggest problems with taking standardized tests is the stress that goes along with it. But don't worry about it! Here are a few tips to help keep stress at a minimum.

1. Always remember that it's just a test.

This is a test. This is only a test. Despite all the myths you may have heard, these tests alone do not determine your future. You've probably heard the horror stories that go something like this: There was this brilliant guy in high school, and he could have gone to any college he wanted, but for some reason he choked on his SATs and didn't get accepted to any of his top choices. Stuff like that just doesn't happen. Colleges are a lot smarter than that, and they won't deny you admission based on a single test score. Also, as we mention later, you can retake them—if you're really disappointed, there is still hope.

2. Relax—it isn't as big of a deal as it may seem.

You need to remember that this is just one test out of hundreds that you will take in your high school career, so it is obviously not worth worrying to death about. Also, everything you need to know to do well on these tests has already been taught to you at some point in high school or even middle school. This means that you don't have to learn any new material to do well; you simply have to take the time to review and study what you've already learned.

3. Colleges look at much more than just your test scores.

Along with relaxing, you should remember that a single test will not determine where you are accepted for college. For some reason, many people seem to think that colleges accept applicants based solely on test scores and GPA. But this is simply not true. On the contrary, these simple numbers are only a small portion of what colleges look at when deciding whom to accept. They also look at what classes you've taken to see if you've challenged yourself. They look at extracurricular activities, including sports, fine arts, membership in clubs, community involvement, and so on. Colleges also understand that some people just aren't good test takers, and they won't hold that against you.

Although standardized tests should be taken seriously, they alone will not have a tremendous impact on college admission.

4. If you don't do well the first time, try, try again.

One of the neat things about the ACT and SAT is that you can take them as many times as you want. Even better, most schools have a policy of taking your highest score. The tests are offered every few months, so one advantage of starting early (during your junior year) is that you can take them several times if you need to work your way up to a good score. (Check out the section on retaking the tests at the end of this chapter.)

Preparing Like a Pro

Now that you're relaxed, you can begin to prepare for the tests. Every test is different, and you will have to prepare for them differently.

Especially in the case of the SAT-like test (compared to the AP tests), you will spend study time differently. To do well on the SAT, you may need to take a preparatory class or maybe just find a book or a software program you can do at home. The PSAT also prepares you for the SAT.

The AP exams, however, are focused on a certain area and are designed to find out how much you know as compared to students everywhere. If your teacher spent too much time on a certain subject, you need to make sure that you know everything else as well, because your teacher will not be making or grading the test. Preparing for the AP exams is much like preparing for any big test in a class: you have to study. There's no way around it; if you really want to score well you have to take time to study. Many study aids can help you, so just set aside some time to review everything.

1. Study with your friends.

Never underestimate the power of group study. Obviously, this doesn't mean that you should invite a huge group of people over, play the music really loud, watch some TV, and mess around. Keep the study group to a manageable size, and make sure that you really study. Remember the old saying, "Two heads are better than one." By sharing your ideas, you can get a lot more accomplished than if you were by yourself. Each of your friends may have different strengths, too, so by combining your knowledge you will learn a lot more and will be strong in more areas. Also, friends are often the best teachers because they can explain stuff in a way you'll understand. Sometimes teachers just can't figure out a simple way to explain things—that's what friends are for.

2. TAKE PRACTICE TESTS.

This can be done within your group study or individually. Either way is helpful, so if you find the time, try both. In a group, after everyone takes the practice test you can go over the answers; the people who got certain problems right can explain how they got the answer to those that got it wrong. This goes back to friends being the best teachers. If you got an answer wrong and you can't figure out why, one of your friends might be able to explain it to you.

By taking the test individually, you can better simulate testing conditions. Plus, after taking it and scoring yourself, you can get a rough idea of how you will do on the actual test.

If, after taking a practice test, you score much lower than you would've liked, don't be discouraged. Many people will tell you that practice tests are often harder than the actual test.

3. LEARN FROM YOUR MISTAKES.

Another reason that taking a practice test is a good idea is that you figure out what types of problems you need to work on. It may be those dreaded analogies, or reading comprehension questions, or certain types of math problems. Whatever it is, practice tests will help you discover which areas you need to practice. Study those areas more thoroughly, doing practice problems similar to the ones that gave you trouble.

> *I found it extremely helpful to take practice tests and then check my answers with a group of friends. Each of us took our own tests under test conditions that allowed only the specified time for each section. Then*

> *we checked our answers together. This was very useful*
> *because it allowed all of us to teach and assist each*
> *other. If I did not understand an answer for a certain*
> *problem, one of my friends who understood it would*
> *show me how he or she figured it out.*
>
> —Brian, Free State High School, Lawrence, Kansas

4. Find some good prep books.

So many books deal with test preparation that it's hard to know where to begin. Entire books are devoted to the ACT, SAT, and PSAT separately. There are also books for each AP subject. Your school probably has a number of them, so ask your teacher or counselor. If not, bookstores everywhere carry preparation books. The best books to get are the ones that have practice tests with explanations of each problem. The explanations are very important, because if you don't know why you missed a problem, chances are you'll miss it (or one like it) again. These books also explain in greater detail the format of the tests and the types of problems that are likely to appear. Some of the AP books also include a summary of the entire subject, which can be used not only for last-minute studying, but also as an aid throughout the year in the AP class you're taking.

5. Improve your vocabulary skills.

A large part of the SAT and ACT tests is based on your knowledge of vocabulary words. It's really hard to answer an analogy or sentence completion question when you don't know what any of the word choices mean! To solve this very common problem, many books have been published that deal solely with learning vocabulary words. Page after page of words that have been on previous tests—and that are likely to show up again (words are often repeated, which is yet another advantage of taking practice tests). Many of the larger preparation books include vocabulary sections as well as practice tests and other useful information. It probably sounds incredibly boring to leaf through a book containing nothing but vocabulary words, but you'll be amazed at how well you remember the words. When test day comes, you'll know it was all worth it when you recognize nearly every word on the test.

6. Use flashcards.

Hey, they worked in elementary school, so why wouldn't they work now? After studying some words, take the ones that give you trouble and make them into flashcards. Sometimes if you're able to visualize the word and its meaning, it will be easier to remember. Companies also sell flashcards, many for vocabulary, but also for math questions, science questions, and every other type of question likely to appear on a test.

The vocabulary flash cards are very helpful. Several types have the word on the front along with a picture. The picture is a visual representation of the word's meaning, so even if you didn't know the word you could guess it by its picture. This really helps because every time you see the word, you remember its picture—and then you'll remember what the word means. On the back of the card, the word is spelled phonetically and is defined. The card also contains a list of synonyms and a list of antonyms. At the bottom, the word is used in a sentence and is used in a possible analogy. If you are generally a visual person and learn better from pictures, flashcards are definitely something you should investigate.

> *When studying for the SAT verbal section, I found it beneficial to use flashcards to memorize words. I went over the cards with another person, and when we were unsure of a word, we would put it in a separate pile to go over again. By doing this, I learned a number of new words, which helped better my understanding of many of the questions on the verbal section.*
>
> —Alison, Free State High School, Lawrence, Kansas

7. Take advantage of computer technology.

Along with books and flashcards, preparation software is available for standardized tests. Some of the software can be bought as a supplement to books, while some covers everything by itself. Taking practice tests on the computer is easier because the computer scores it for you, which saves a lot of time. However, on the real tests you actually have to fill in those little ovals with your number 2 pencil, so keep that in mind if you're timing yourself. Also, software is available for vocabulary. If books and flashcards just aren't your thing, try learning all those words on your computer. (Your school counseling office also may have a computer and software for student use.)

Software is also extremely helpful for the AP tests. Software for the AP European History test, for example, has three full-length practice tests, with explanations of not only why a certain answer is correct, but also why every other choice is wrong. The test also includes maps and diagrams to help you study. Preparation software is very useful because it's so quick and easy. Try it—it can't hurt!

8. TAKE A TEST-PREPARATION CLASS.

One option for test preparation is enrolling in a class. Preparation classes are offered for every standardized test, and because many of the tests are similar, some prepare you for several of them at the same time. Classes are offered throughout the entire year, so talk to your counselors and teachers to find one that fits your schedule. Some classes may be school-related, while others are not.

> *Preparing for standardized tests is very important for achieving a good score. An excellent way to prepare is to take a prep course. My sophomore year, my school offered an SAT prep course that I found very helpful. It made me familiar with test-taking strategies and improved my vocabulary. When the test day came, I knew that I was ready.*
>
> —LAURA, GREGORY-PORTLAND HIGH SCHOOL, PORTLAND, TEXAS

A typical summer preparation class is two to three weeks long and meets four or five times a week. During the school year, classes are generally offered once or twice a week for a few months. Obviously, this will depend on your school. These classes are very helpful if you want to learn some test-taking strategies and tips. Also, by taking a class, you are forced to set aside time to study for the test, so you can't just put off studying until the last minute. These classes incorporate many of the preparation tips already mentioned, including preparation books, vocabulary books, group study, taking practice tests, and software use. Depending on who runs the course, these classes can be pretty pricey, but if it will help you get the score you want, it is probably worth the investment. Shop around first, and ask counselors and older students for advice.

> *I strongly recommend taking an SAT or ACT class to help improve your score. I took a verbal SAT and ACT class. Our school didn't offer a preparation class, so I sought an energetic teacher that would fit my learning style. She made the classes fun, which helped the majority of the students learn the material. She taught us test-taking techniques, such as shortcuts to improve test-taking time, vocabulary, simple grammatical things that are often forgotten, and other methods to improve our scores.*
>
> —TODD, FREE STATE HIGH SCHOOL, LAWRENCE, KANSAS

9. READ OUTSIDE OF SCHOOL.

Novels, magazines, short stories, poetry, the newspaper—read anything at all. Reading is the number one way to improve your vocabulary, and because so much of any test is based on vocabulary, this will improve your score. By reading, you'll learn words without even realizing that you're learning them because you'll be able to guess their meanings from their context. Or, if there's that occasional word that you just can't figure out, look it up in a dictionary. There's another word you'll know on the test.

Now that you have some ideas on how to prepare for the tests, you just have to figure out when you're going to take them.

When Is the Best Time to Take Each Test?

The AP tests and the PSAT are only offered once a year, so make sure you don't miss the registration deadline—you won't get another chance. Listen for school bulletins, or talk to your counselor or teacher. But with the ACTs and SATs you have a choice. These tests are offered several times throughout the year, so you can choose a time that fits your schedule, a time when you won't be too stressed out with other assignments. (Finals week would probably be a bad time, for example.) Also, seriously consider taking these tests in the spring (if not fall *and* spring) of your junior year instead of waiting until your senior year. If you're pleased with your score, you won't have to take the test your senior year, which will already be busy with the college application process. And if you didn't do as well as you would have liked, you have the option of retaking the tests.

Retaking the SAT and ACT

As stated earlier, one of the best things about the ACT and SAT is the possibility of retaking either of these tests if you are not pleased with your first score. It may cost a few extra bucks, but in the long run it will probably be to your benefit. Most colleges look only at your highest scores, so retaking the tests can only help you. For example, pretend that you planned ahead and took the SAT your junior year. You were very pleased with your math score, but you felt that your verbal score needed some improvement. You studied over the summer and took the test again your senior year. This time your verbal score was excellent, but for some reason your math score dropped (this is not uncommon). When reviewing your scores, colleges would look at your math score from the first test and your verbal score from the second test. Aren't you glad you decided to retake the test?

Finishing Up

Standardized tests are a necessary evil in the life of every high school student; we hope that the tips in this chapter will give you the confidence and skills you need to put the demon of standardized tests to rest.

CHAPTER 25

The College Application Process

> When I was in eighth grade, I walked into my advisor's room because I was early to school and really bored. That year, my advisor was also the English teacher for my grade, so she had tons of books lying around. I picked one up because it had a cool picture on the cover, and I looked at what it was. It was a book of college application essays. Not exactly a wake-up call at 7:00 a.m., but I figured I might as well give it a go. I read this one essay, which I don't even remember except that it was about a fly and how we are all like a fly in some ways. I don't know why, but that really stuck with me, and I have been planning my own essay ever since.
>
> —MERRITT, HERITAGE HIGH SCHOOL, LITTLETON, COLORADO

Applying to college can be an overwhelming process, but it doesn't have to be a problem if you are focused, organized, and motivated. The college search should begin during your junior year: The earlier you start, the less you will have to worry about it your senior year.

GETTING A HEAD START JUNIOR YEAR

1. GET TO KNOW YOUR GUIDANCE COUNSELOR.

Your guidance counselor is the person who will be writing recommendations for you next year, so make sure you stop in periodically to chat. This will give your counselor a good idea about the kind of person that you are and will make it easy for him or her to write a good recommendation.

2. UNDERSTAND THE COLLEGE ENTRANCE REQUIREMENTS.

Universities will expect you to take diverse classes. How many years of a foreign language should you take? How many more fine arts credits do you need? How many years of science are required? Each university requires different classes, but as a general rule of thumb, the more years of English, math, science, and language you take, the better off you are.

3. PUT TOGETHER A RESUME.

Make a list of your extracurricular activities, special achievements, honors, awards, community service, and school involvement. It might look something like this:

> Johnnie Overachiever
> 123 Egotrip Lane
> Imsocool, Oregon 93452
>
> Studmuffin High School
> Cumulative GPA: 4.36 (weighted)
>
> **Activities and Offices Held**
>
> 1998–Present, USY Regional President (Pacific Northwest Region encompasses Washington, Oregon, Idaho, Montana, Alaska, British Columbia, and Northern Alberta)
>
> 1998–Present, Board Member, Senate Advisory Youth Involvement Team (Say It!)

1998–Present, Member, Senior Service Club

1998–Present, President of National Honor Society

1998, Planned leadership convention attended by 100 teenagers

1997–Present, Literacy Corps, volunteering twice weekly in two inner-city Seattle schools

1996–Present, Staff Writer, *The Gator Gazette*

1995–1997, Member, high school basketball team

Honors and Special Awards

1998, Masonic Award

1998, Hilda and Benjamin Asia Academic Excellence Award

1997, 1st place, Media Fest '97, "Beginning Animation"

1996–1997, 1st place for photography, "Reflections"

1996, Youth Hall of Fame

1996, Music Video, Honorable Mention Award

Summer Programs and Special Events Attended

1997, Eastern European Pilgrimage (Traveled to Hungary, Czechoslovakia, Poland, and Israel to study Jewish life before, after, and during WWII)

1996, USY on Wheels (Traveled by bus around the entire United States with 45 other teenagers)

Special Experiences and Hobbies

1997, Produced a video for the Studmuffin School Foundation, documenting the elementary, middle, and high schools. Shown to the community to raise money for school supplies.

1996–Present, Member, Cascade Juggler's Club

Okay, so your resume might not look something like this—but it's cool that not everyone is a Johnnie Overachiever (thank goodness). Still, there has to be some interesting stuff that you are going to want to let colleges know about yourself, and putting that stuff into resume format can be a big help. Generally, you should keep your resume to under a page, if possible—and certainly no more than two pages.

4. LOOK THROUGH COLLEGE GUIDES.

Now is the time to familiarize yourself with different colleges. Your school's counseling center is a great place to find college guidebooks. Start to think about what interests you and the possible majors you would like to pursue—not because you will need to decide that kind of thing anytime soon, but because certain schools will probably be more attractive to you if you know the general areas that interest you.

5. FIND OUT ABOUT TEST DATES.

Find out about taking the PSAT/NMSQT tests in October. By doing well on these tests, you make yourself eligible for awards and scholarships. Also consider taking the SAT II subject tests while the material is still fresh in your mind. There are 24 different subject tests in 18 subjects, so find a subject in which you are confident. It's also a good idea to take an SAT I test toward the end of the year. The sign-up dates for these tests will be early, so make sure that you sign up on time because late fees apply to students who register after the deadline. (Check out Chapter 24, "Preparing for Standardized Tests.")

6. READ THE COLLEGE BROCHURES YOU RECEIVE IN THE MAIL.

If you take the PSAT in the fall, then you will be receiving tons of mail from colleges. Read through them and consider qualities such as these:

Where in the country is the college located?

Is it affiliated with a religion?

How much is tuition?

Is it in your state or out of state?

What classes are offered?

What does it specialize in?

How large is it?

Is it in a big city or a college town?

These questions will be important later when you are deciding on which schools to apply to. Gather these brochures in one location, such as a manila envelope, file folder, or file cabinet. Make sure that they are all in one place so that you can easily refer back to them.

GETTING CLOSER! YOUR PLAN FOR THE SUMMER BEFORE SENIOR YEAR

1. TRY TO VISIT CAMPUSES THAT INTEREST YOU.

After reading through the college pamphlets that you receive in the mail, looking up schools in college guides, and talking with your parents, plan a trip to visit the schools that interest you. The purpose of these tours is to give you a flavor of campus life; each campus has its own architecture and personality. Sometimes you can go on a college trip through your school with a group of students and an advisor. These trips are famous for visiting the greatest amount of schools in the least amount of time. Remember that summer is a busy time for college visits, so you may need to arrange a tour at least two weeks ahead before visiting.

2. CHECK OUT YOUR RESOURCES AT COLLEGES.

Sometimes you can interview with an admissions representative if an interview is recommended or required, but you will definitely need to call ahead to make an appointment if you want to do this.

You can find the number for the admissions office by looking it up on the Internet, consulting guidebooks, or reading a college catalogue. When you call, make sure you arrange a tour of the campus, faculties, and a dorm tour (if available), and schedule a visit to classes of interest or a meeting with professors or coaches.

3. MAKE A LIST OF INTERESTING SCHOOLS.

Make a list of around 10 schools that interest you. After you make the list, you should have an idea about which geographic location most of your schools are in, the size of the school you are looking for, and maybe even which courses you are interested in.

4. REQUEST APPLICATIONS.

If you have the catalogs for all the schools that you want to apply to, you will find a phone number or a reply card inside each for requesting applications.

For an even easier route, nearly every school has a Web page. You can find these Internet addresses in any college guide, or go to: http://www.clas.ufl.edu/clas/american-universities.html for information. At this site you'll find a listing of American colleges and universities. You can download many applications from http://www.collegelink.com.

Request applications from all the schools on your list, even if they're not your first choice. Usually schools begin to send out applications in September, so make sure you are on their mailing lists. It generally takes anywhere from two to four weeks to receive an application after you request it, so start early. If you do not get one, then you should call the admissions office of the school and request an application by phone.

5. USE OTHER RESOURCES.

Many online resources are available for learning about colleges:

- http://www.ctown.com
- http://www.tpoint.net/~jewels/college.html
- http://www.sourcepath.com
- http://www.collegeboard.org
- http://www.collegenet.com/cnmain.html

SENIOR YEAR: REACHING THE SUMMIT

1. TAKE THE STANDARDIZED TESTS.

If you haven't already, this year you will be taking the SAT I's, SAT II's, and (possibly) AP exams. Turn to Chapter 24 to find out more about preparing for these tests.

2. MAKE SURE THAT THE CLASSES YOU TAKE ARE ACADEMICALLY CHALLENGING.

Many students believe the myth that their senior year will be the easiest. "I've worked hard for three years, and it's time to take a break." Wrong! You must continue to work hard your senior year. Take the core classes such as English, math, science, and a foreign language. Your transcript should show that you are continuing to work hard your senior year. (At least during the first semester—*senioritis* may be unavoidable that spring!)

3. WRITE YOUR APPLICATION ESSAY.

Look at the applications to the schools you are interested in, and find out what questions they ask. The most common topics include these:

- Write about someone who has made an impact on your life.

- Illustrate one or more themes, events, or individuals that have helped to shape you.

- Why do you want to go to this school?

- What characteristics can you bring to the campus?

- Describe a particular event and the lesson that you learned from it.

Find Your Topic

The earlier you find out the question, the more time you have to attack your essay. Start by writing the essay question at the top of a 3-by-5-inch note card. Carry these note cards around with you, and write down possible answers to the questions. Later, narrow the list by crossing off ideas that you cannot write at least one page about. When you finally have your topic, write down an outline of the ideas you want to cover. The essay is usually limited to around 500 words, or about a page and a half, double-spaced.

Approach the essay by finding a topic that excites you so that you can really bring your essay to life. Be sure to write about what the question asks, because an admissions officer will notice if you don't. At the same time, however, don't be afraid to be creative—you want to be the one that stands out!

Write a Draft

When you have decided how you want to approach the question, write a first draft. Put the essay away for a few days, then read it again. Does it flow? Does it make sense? Is it interesting?

This is the one part of the application that lets you be yourself and shine, so work hard on it. Neil Simon wrote, "The writing of a book should destroy the writer. If there is anything left, he has not worked hard enough." The same is true for the college application. After you are satisfied with your essay, take it to school and ask some of your teachers to read it. These will be your best editors. As a representative from UCLA said, "Rewrite your essay 500 times. Then rewrite it again."

GET YOUR RECOMMENDERS, AND THEN GET YOUR RECOMMENDATIONS

Think about which teacher(s) you want to write recommendations for you. Most colleges will require at least one recommendation from a teacher. Depending on how many schools you apply to, choose one or two teachers who know you well and have a good idea of your strengths and personality. In deciding which teachers to ask, think about how long and how well each of your teachers knows you. It is a good idea to ask teachers from your junior year because they are the teachers who have taught you most recently for a full year.

Ask Your Teachers

It is polite to ask your teachers if they would be willing to write a recommendation before you give them the recommendation forms. Allow as much time as possible—and at least two weeks—between the time you give your teacher the recommendation and the date it is due.

If you are asking a teacher to write a recommendation for more than one school, you might want to put all the forms and preaddressed envelopes in one file folder. As an added favor, you can write the name of each school and the due date on the outside of the folder. Make sure to highlight the important information on each form, such as deadlines, the school(s) you are applying to, and whether they should be mailed or given to the counselor.

Follow Up: People Can Forget

A few days before deadline time, follow up with the person writing the recommendation to make sure that he or she remembers. It is not rude to remind your recommenders, but you can preface your remin-der by saying "I know you're really busy, so I just wanted to remind you. . . ."

Don't Forget a Thank-You

It is important to thank your teachers for writing your recommendation. Teachers are swamped with recommendations, so it might be nice to give them a gift around the holiday season to thank them for their time. Even a nice short note will be much appreciated.

FIND OUT ABOUT FINANCIAL AID

Check your counseling center and library for books and pamphlets about financial aid. Look for state, federal, and local programs that apply to you. If there are any private programs that you want to apply for, get all the forms necessary and fill them out. Usually, these scholarship opportunities have early deadlines. You also can check out many good Web sites to find out about financial aid:

- http://www.collegeboard.org
- http://www.finaid.org
- http://www.finaid.org/nasfa
- http://www.studentservices.com/fastweb

HOW TO CALM INTERVIEW ANXIETIES

If the school you are visiting grants interviews, or if you are interviewing with an alumni representative near home, here are a few hints to help you feel comfortable.

Before You Go to the Interview

- Make a list of questions you want to know the answers to, the ones that aren't covered in the pamphlets you receive. You can ask about internship opportunities, travel abroad, out-of-state acceptance, and campus clubs.

- Have your parents or friends ask you questions they think the interviewer will ask. This will give you practice talking about your test scores, grades, extracurricular actives, and your interest in the college.

At the Interview

- Be early to the interview. You will look better walking in and having a cup of coffee than running in the office in a rush.

- Dress neatly. Guys should wear a collared shirt that can be tucked in, formal pants, and dress shoes. Girls should wear a dress or a formal shirt and pants.

- Relax! Be yourself and have fun. Pretend *you* are interviewing *them!* Be enthusiastic and give thoughtful answers.

- Afterward, remember to firmly shake your interviewer's hand, look him or her in the eyes, and say thank-you.

FINAL THOUGHTS

Finish your applications as soon as possible! The sooner you finish the application, the better you'll feel. Good luck!

ABOUT THE AUTHORS

CARTOONIST

Kerin Lubetich

High School: Mercer Island High School, Mercer Island, Washington

Activities: Intramural volleyball, ballet, school murals, modern dance, water-skiing, steel drum band member, journalism, newspaper illustrator and writer

Best Piece of Advice: "If you are unhappy with the way you look now, imagine how you're going to feel at seventy-five."

CO-AUTHORS

Christine Anneberg

High School: Phillips Academy, Andover, Massachusetts

Activities: Field hockey, basketball, lacrosse, community service

Best Piece of Advice: Remember this famous Latin adage, "Si hoc legere scis nimium eruditionis habes!" Translation: "If you can read this, you're overeducated!"

Merritt Baer

High School: Heritage High School, Littleton, Colorado

Activities: Soccer, field hockey, basketball, choir, photography, community service

Best Piece of Advice: "Out beyond ideas of wrongdoing and rightdoing there is a field. I'll meet you there."

Peter Baer

High School: Heritage High School, Littleton, Colorado

Activities: Soccer, lacrosse, basketball, community service, student government

Best Piece of Advice: "Aspire to achieve balance. School is important, but remember it's only school."

LAUREN BAUM

High School: Isadore Newman High School, New Orleans, Louisiana

Activities: Captain of the cross-country and track teams

Best Piece of Advice: "Work hard, play hard."

MARC BRIDGE

High School: Mercer Island High School, Mercer Island, Washington

Activities: Sports broadcasting, tennis, skiing, baseball enthusiast

Best Piece of Advice: "Wherever you go, there you are."

LEAH CARNICK

High School: Chapel Hill High School, Chapel Hill, North Carolina

Activities: Photography, listening to music, having a good time with my friends

Best Piece of Advice: "For every hand extended another lies in wait. Keep your eye on that one, anticipate."—Ani DiFranco

MICHAEL CARNICK

High School: Torrey Pines High School, Del Mar, California

Activities: Computer graphics, game design, writing

Best Piece of Advice: "When life gives you lemons . . . throw them at your neighbor."

ANNIE CHU

School: Mercer Island High School, Mercer Island, Washington

Activities: Tennis, National Honor Society, DECA, Youth Hall of Fame

Best Piece of Advice: "Never let a ding in the windshield distract your vision of the road ahead."

STEPHANIE CURRY

High School: Mercer Island High School, Mercer Island, Washington

Activities: Choir, drama, skiing, photography, crew

Best Piece of Advice: "When you get to the end of your rope, tie a knot and hang on."—F.D.R.

JENNIFER DER YUEN

High School: Mercer Island High School, Mercer Island, Washington

Activities: Crew, skiing, national charities league, student government, job

Best Piece of Advice: "I am easily satisfied with the best."—Winston Churchill

MIRIAM D'JAEN

High School: Mercer Island High School, Mercer Island, Washington

Activities: Dance, tutoring inner-city kids, teaching dance, tennis

Best Piece of Advice: "Put your face towards the sunshine and you cannot see the shadows."—Helen Keller

MICHAEL HAZEL

High School: Free State High School, Kansas

Activities: Soccer, basketball, Model United Nations, piano, Spanish club

Best Piece of Advice: "The future is no place to place your better days."—Dave Matthews

MEREDITH HIGASHI

High School: Mercer Island High School, Mercer Island, Washington

Activities: School newspaper, National Honor Society, tennis, handbell choir, youth group, piano

Best Piece of Advice: "When we put a limit on what we do, we put a limit on what we can do."—Charles Schwab

SHANNON HOPKINS

High School: George Washington High School, Denver, Colorado

Activities: Field hockey, soccer, literary magazine, mountaineering club, piano, Volunteers for Outdoor Colorado Advisory board member

Best Piece of Advice: "Smile, it gets you far in life!"

PALMER JOSEPH (PJ) HOYT

High School: Grangeville High School, Grangeville, Idaho

Activities: Year exchange to Switzerland, National Ski Patrolman, football, baseball, student government, choir, school musical

Best Piece of Advice: "I hope life isn't just one big joke, 'cause man, I don't get it."

JULIE MALLORY

High School: Heritage High School, Littleton, Colorado

Activities: Tennis, piano, Key Club, National Honor Society, Model United Nations

Best Piece of Advice: "Minds are like parachutes. They only function when open."

SUSAN RINDLAUB

High School: Mercer Island High School

Activities: Volleyball, basketball, tennis, listening to music, hanging out with friends, playing the piano, eating, being with millog

Best Piece of Advice: "Whatever you want to do, do it today, there will only be so many tomorrows."

CASEY ROSE

High School: Mililani High School, Mililani, Hawaii

Activities: Track, football, speech/debate, National Honor Society

Best Piece of Advice: "When in doubt, go to the beach."

SARAH MICHELLE SHULMAN

High School: Mercer Island High School, Mercer Island, Washington

Activities: Swim team, student government, National Honor Society, community service, journalism, photography, debate

Best Piece of Advice: "Put yourself out there and let teachers do their magic by getting to know you as a person and as a student."

KATE SOMMERS-DAWES

High School: Saint Mary's Hall, San Antonio, Texas

Activities: Ballet, singing, drama, horseback riding

Best Piece of Advice: "Reach for the moon—you'll end up among the stars."

ORLANDO TIRADO

High School: San Dieguito Academy, Encinitas, California

Activities: Photojournalism, poetry, newspaper, painting, human rights activism

Best Piece of Advice: "Become active physically and emotionally. It will get rid of casual boredom and give you somewhere to go, something to look forward to."

Jason Uhrmacher

High School: Mercer Island High School, Mercer Island, Washington

Activities: USY Pinwheel Regional President, *Mirror Magazine* staff writer, tennis, Managing Editor—*Mercer High Times*, Literacy Corps volunteer, Mercer Island High School Seinfeld Club co-founder.

Best Piece of Advice: "We are what we repeatedly do. Excellence, then, is not an art, but a habit."—Aristotle

Ajay Vashee

High School: Mercer Island High School, Mercer Island, Washington

Activities: Tennis, mountain biking, piano

Best Piece of Advice: "Time you spend doing homework is just as important as time you spend relaxing."